Wei-Chiang Hong

KV-060-755

Competitiveness in the Tourism Sector

A Comprehensive Approach from Economic and Management Points

Physica-Verlag

A Springer Company

Prof. Wei-Chiang Hong
Department of Information
Management
Oriental Institute of Technology
58 Sec. 2, Sichuan Rd.
Panchiao, Taipei, 220
Taiwan
samuelhong@ieee.org

ISBN: 978-3-7908-2041-6   e-ISBN: 978-3-7908-2042-3

Contributions to Economics ISSN: 1431-1933

Library of Congress Control Number: 2008923546

© 2008 Physica-Verlag Heidelberg

This work is subject to copyright. All rights are reserved, whether the whole or part of the material is concerned, specifically the rights of translation, reprinting, reuse of illustrations, recitation, broadcasting, reproduction on microfilm or in any other way, and storage in data banks. Duplication of this publication or parts thereof is permitted only under the provisions of the German Copyright Law of September 9, 1965, in its current version, and permission for use must always be obtained from Springer. Violations are liable to prosecution under the German Copyright Law.

The use of general descriptive names, registered names, trademarks, etc. in this publication does not imply, even in the absence of a specific statement, that such names are exempt from the relevant protective laws and regulations and therefore free for general use.

Cover design: WMXDesign GmbH, Heidelberg

Printed on acid-free paper

9 8 7 6 5 4 3 2 1

springer.com

5001336927

WITHDRAWN

Competitiveness in the Tourism Sector

Contributions to Economics

www.springer.com/series/1262

Further volumes of this series can be found at our homepage

Russel Cooper/Gary Madden/
Ashley Lloyd/Michael Schipp (Eds.)
**The Economics of Online Markets
and ICI Networks**
2006. ISBN 978-3-7908-1706-5

Renato Giannetti/Michelangelo Vasta (Eds.)
**Evolution of Italian Enterprises
in the 20th Century**
2006. ISBN 978-3-7908-1711-9

Ralph Setzer
**The Politics of Exchange Rates
in Developing Countries**
2006. ISBN 978-3-7908-1715-7

Dora Borbély
**Trade Specialization in the Enlarged
European Union**
2006. ISBN 978-3-7908-1704-1

Iris A. Hauswirth
Effective and Efficient Organisations?
2006. ISBN 978-3-7908-1730-0

Marco Neuhaus
The Impact of FDI on Economic Growth
2006. ISBN 978-3-7908-1734-8

Nicola Jentzsch
**The Economics and Regulation
of Financial Privacy**
2006. ISBN 978-3-7908-1737-9

Klaus Winkler
**Negotiations with Asymmetrical
Distribution of Power**
2006. ISBN 978-3-7908-1743-0

Sasha Isenkova, Zorica Nedović-Budić
(Eds.)
The Urban Mosaic of Post-Socialist Europe
2006. ISBN 978-3-7908-1726-3

Brigitte Preissl/Jürgen Müller (Eds.)
Governance of Communication Networks
2006. ISBN 978-3-7908-1745-4[-6pt]
Lei Delsen/Derek Bosworth/Hermann Groß
Rafael Muñoz de Bustillo y Llorente (Eds.)
Operating Hours and Working Times
2006. ISBN 978-3-7908-1759-1

Pablo Coto-Millán; Vicente Inglada (Eds.)
Essays on Transport Economics
2006. ISBN 978-3-7908-1764-5

Christian H. Fahrholz
**New Political Economy of Exchange Rate
Policies and the Enlargement of the**

Eurozone
2006. ISBN 978-3-7908-1761-4

Sandra Gruescu
Population Ageing and Economic Growth
2007. ISBN 978-3-7908-1905-2

Patrick S. Renz
Project Governance
2007. ISBN 978-3-7908-1926-7

Christian Schabbel
The Value Chain of Foreign Aid
2007. ISBN 978-3-7908-1931-1

Martin Eckardt
Insurance Intermediation
2007. ISBN 978-3-7908-1939-7

George M. Korres (Ed.)
**Regionalisation, Growth,
and Economic Integration**
2007. ISBN 978-3-7908-1924-3

Kerstin Groß
Equity Ownership and Performance
2007. ISBN 978-3-7908-1933-5

Ulrike Neyer
**The Design of the Eurosystem's Monetary
Policy Instruments**
2007. ISBN 978-3-7908-1977-9

Christian Roland
Banking Sector Liberalization in India
2008. ISBN 978-3-7908-1981-6

Nicole Brunhart
**Individual Financial Planning
for Retirement**
2008. ISBN 978-3-7908-1997-7

Bas van Aarle/Klaus Weyerstrass (Eds)
**Economic Spillovers, Structural Reforms
and Policy Coordination in the Euro Area**
2008. ISBN 978-3-7908-1969-4

Karin Luger
Chinese Railways
2008. ISBN 978-3-7908-2001-0

Christina Keinert
**Corporate Social Responsibility
as an International Strategy**
2008. ISBN 978-3-7908-2023-2

Petr Pavlínek
A Successful Transformation?
2008. ISBN 978-3-7908-2039-3

Wei-Chiang Hong
Competitiveness in the Tourism Sector
2008. ISBN 978-3-7908-2041-6

Acknowledgements

I AM DEEPLY INDEBTED to my advisors, Professor Robert Theng and Professor Ping-Feng Pai, whose patient guidance, stimulating encouragement, and deep insights in research have helped me immeasurably throughout the course of my dissertation research. They guided me into the exciting forecasting areas and national/industrial competitiveness evaluation system constructing. Their valuable suggestions and experiments helped me identify the suitable research topic and always keep in the development frontier of international academy. This dissertation would never have been written without their kind and patient assistances.

Meanwhile, I would like to thank the National Science Council (NSC, Taiwan) to sponsor me, by the Graduate Student Study Abroad Program (GSSAP; sponsor series no.: 095-2917-I-212-001), as a visiting scholar in the Institute of Scientific and Industrial Research, Osaka University, Japan. During the 7-month visiting period, Professor Hiroshi Motoda, Professor Takashi Washio, and Professor Kouzou Ohara also kindly introduced me lots of new direction tracks in the machine learning field, this is an abundant visiting journey.

I truly appreciate the friendship of my friends and colleagues in the Ph.D. Program for having created a pleasant working environment and for helpful discussions. Special thanks go to Professor Chen-Tung Chen, Professor Ching-Torng Lin, Professor Ruey-Ming Chao, Professor Hown-wen Chen, Professor Dong-Yih Bau, Dr. Shao-Lun Lee, Dr. Peng-Wen Chen, Dr. Chien-Yuan Lai, Dr. Yi-Hsien Wu, Dr. Yi-Hsuan Yeh, Dr. Wan-Kuang Hsieh, and Professor Lawrence W. Lan, respectively, for their many hours of instruction and guidance in my earliest courage stage of Ph.D. Program research and graduate research.

In addition, I'll be responsible for all details in this dissertation, of course, I'd like to receive any constructive suggestion if existing any controversial issue, rather than unmeaning wording. While I listened attentively to the "Past Anecdotes" of France Royals from the short-fat tourist guide of Chateau de Versailles and Louvre, impression in my mind is not only his detailing commentates, but also his showing responsible for his job and proud of his country. I think this is the key successful factor that a great nation would remain its competitiveness and become unshakeable as time goes by.

Finally, I owe my deepest appreciation to my parents Mr. Hsien-Long Hong and Mrs. Hsu-Fang Chen, brothers Mr. Wei-Mo Hong and Mr. Wei-Yang Hong for their steady support and endless love. In the meanwhile, I would like to express my sincere gratitude to my beloved wife Mrs. Su-Mei Tsai for her deepest love and taking care of our cute-clever son Chang-Hsin, constant understanding, and being together with me in the whole research journey. All of them have always been a source of inspiration. Without their support through these years, I would not be able to afford the luxury of pursuing my own research interests.

Contents

Abbreviations IX

1 Introduction... 1
  1.1 Competition in the Tourism Industry 1
    1.1.1 Domestic-Perspective Competition 1
    1.1.2 International-Perspective Competition 2
    1.1.3 Summary 3
  1.2 Motivation 4
    1.2.1 Perspectives on Competitiveness.............................. 4
    1.2.2 Competitiveness Evaluations.................................. 5
    1.2.3 Summary 6
  1.3 Problem Statement.. 7
    1.3.1 Evolution of Competitiveness 7
    1.3.2 Composition of Tourism Competitiveness 9
  1.4 Contributions 10
  References 12

2 Literature Reviews..19
  2.1 Exogenous Comparative Advantage Theory 20
    2.1.1 Enlightenment of Adam Smith's Absolute Advantage 20
    2.1.2 Introduction and Discussion 21
    2.1.3 Summary 22
  2.2 Endogenous Comparative Advantage Theory 22
    2.2.1 Specialization Processes.................................... 23
    2.2.2 Technological Innovation 25
    2.2.3 Summary 25
  2.3 Competitive Advantages... 26
    2.3.1 Introduction 26
    2.3.2 Debates, Adjusted Models, and Successors.................... 29
    2.3.3 Summary 32
  2.4 Competitiveness and Evaluation Methodology 33
    2.4.1 Definitions of Competitiveness 33
    2.4.2 Evaluation Methodology 37

2.5 Tourism Competitiveness Researches 43
   2.5.1 Overview of Tourism Competitiveness Researches 43
   2.5.2 Crouch and Ritchie's Contributions 45
References 47

3 Research Methods 53
3.1 Evaluative Indicators for Tourism Competitive Information 53
   3.1.1 Comparative Advantages 54
   3.1.2 Competitive Advantages 58
   3.1.3 Tourism Management 63
   3.1.4 Environment Conditions 67
3.2 Influential Effects of Tourism Competitive Information 70
   3.2.1 RCA-Originated Influential Effects 70
   3.2.2 PCA-Originated Influential Effects 73
3.3 Evaluation Methodology and Procedure 75
   3.3.1 Evaluation Indicators 76
   3.3.2 AHP to Evaluate Weights of Indicators 76
References 85

4 Weight of Indicators and Decision Analyses 89
4.1 AHP Questionnaire Survey Procedure 89
4.2 Weight of Indicators Analysis 90
   4.2.1 Weight Analysis on Principal Evaluation Dimensions 90
   4.2.2 Weight Analysis on Comparative Advantages 91
   4.2.3 Weight Analysis on Competitive Advantages 93
   4.2.4 Weight Analysis on Tourism Management 95
   4.2.5 Weight Analysis on Environment Conditions 96
4.3 Statistical Analyses and Feasible Decisions Considerations 98
References 101

5 Conclusions and Future Works 103
5.1 Conclusions 103
5.2 Future Works 106
Reference 106

Appendix 107

Abbreviations

AHP:	Analytic Hierarchy Process
APEC:	Asia-Pacific Economic Cooperation
DEA:	Data Envelopment Analysis
FDI:	Foreign Direct Investment
FTA:	Free Trade Agreement
GCR:	Global Competitiveness Report (published by WEF)
IMD:	International Institute for Management Development
IMF:	International Monetary Fund
KDD:	Knowledge Discovery in Databases
NIS:	National Innovation Systems
OECD:	Organization for Economic Co-Operation and Development
OOPEC:	Office for Official Publications of the European Communities
PCA:	Porter's Competitive Advantages Framework
PCT:	Product Cycle Theory
RCA:	Ricardian Comparative Advantages Theory (including endogenous comparative advantages and exogenous comparative advantages)
R&D:	Research and Development
TDI:	Tourism Destination Image
UN:	United Nations
UNESCO:	United Nations Educational, Scientific and Cultural Organization
UNWTO:	United Nations World Tourism Organization
WCY:	World Competitiveness Yearbook (published by IMD)

WEF:	World Economic Forum
WTC:	World Trade Center
WTO:	World Trade Organization
WTTC:	World Travel and Tourism Council
WWW:	World Wide Web

1 Introduction

1.1 Competition in the Tourism Industry

Tourism has emerged as one of the largest and the fastest growing industries worldwide in the twentieth century (UNWTO,[1] 2005; WTTC, 2005). For example, although depressed reaction of the Iraq war and SARS in 2003, global international tourist receipts in 2004 were still around US$623 billion (with a double-digit growth rate of 18.8%) from an estimated 763 million tourists (UNWTO, 2005), despite the reaction to the Iraq war and SARS in 2003. Additionally, the World Travel & Tourism Council (WTTC) predicted that, global tourism output in 2005 would amount to approximately US$ 6.2 trillion, representing 10.6% of world economic output, and 221 million jobs in tourism, representing some 8.3% of worldwide employment. The tourism sector is optimistically over the next decade to realize a real growth rate of output approximately 4.6%, reaching US$ 10.7 trillion by the year 2015. Tourism's share of global economic output and worldwide employment is expected to reach 11.3% and 8.9%, respectively (WTTC, 2005), in the next 10 years. Due to these great contributions to economic growth, the tourism industry and its related issues have received strong attention, particularly on competitiveness issue. The competitivity of the tourism industry can be illustrated from two perspectives, domestic and international.

1.1.1 Domestic-Perspective Competition

The tourism industry, which benefits the domestic transportation, accommodation, catering, entertainment, and retailing sectors, has social, cultural, and political significance, and makes the following substantial contributions to the economy (APEC Tourism Charter, 2000),

---

[1] Since December 1, 2005, **WTO** (the abbreviation of World Tourism Organization) had changed to **UNWTO** (United Nations World Tourism Organization). See website linkage: http://www.world-tourism.org/newsroom/Releases/2005/december/acronym.htm.

W.-C. Hong, *Competitiveness in the Tourism Sector.* Contributions to Economics,
doi: 10.1007/978-3-7908-2042-3_1, © Physica-Verlag Heidelberg 2008

1. It is a key source of economic demand and growth in demand.
2. It is a major employer at all economic levels, generating of sustainable employment opportunities.
3. It is a significant earner of foreign exchange.
4. It is an important generator of business opportunities for small and medium sized enterprises.
5. It disperses economic benefits within and between economies, particularly at the provincial level.
6. It contributes significantly to the achievement of governments' economic and fiscal goals.
7. It is a catalyst for partnership between the public and private sectors.

Therefore, worldwide tourism expenditure has become an important source of economic activity, employment, tax revenue, income and foreign exchange. Many countries and regions that rely on tourism, such as Caribbean, Mediterranean, Latin American, Southeast Asian countries (Dharmaratne, 1995; Pai & Hong, 2005; Patsouratis, Frangouli & Anastasopoulos, 2005), realizing the expanding significance of the economics of tourism, have begun to channel their resources into its development to enhance their image and attractiveness among global international travelers and tourists (Ritchie & Crouch, 2000). However, not all countries are created equal. Some of them have abundant natural resources (thus have a comparative advantage), while others may have limited naturally landscape, sources, and poor infrastructure. Tourism products, including unfilled airline seats, unoccupied hotel rooms and unused facilities, cannot be stocked because of their transient nature (Archer, 1987).

Hence, an important research issue is to analyze and interpret qualitative and quantitative data to maintain the competitive advantage of a country's tourism industry, compare it with competing destinations. This perspective is based on domestic competition consideration, but competition in tourism is also global.

1.1.2 International-Perspective Competition

Due to the recent trend of globalization,[2] the issue of competitive advantages is important not only to the tourism industry, but also to government

---

[2] At a business level, globalization is referred to "the increasing integration of economies around the world, particularly through trade and financial

and academia. In particular, opening up to trade within the World Trade Organization means that industry, including the tourism industry, can no longer survive through protectionist government policies. Multinational businesses are increasingly moving into domestic markets.

Other factors increasing competitive pressure the progress of telecommunications and information technology, and the increasing sophistication of customers, who demand increasingly high standards from business (Porter, 1990). Businesses have to ensure that their overall attractiveness, and the experiences that they deliver to tourists, at least equal that of many alternatives' experiences open to potential tourists.

Dwyer, Forsyth and Rao (2000, p. 10) wrote "It is useful for the industry and government to understand where a country's competitive position is weakest and strongest." Any tourism businesses (destinations) in each country are compelled to maintain a high level of competitive advantages to withstand these globalization competition pressures.

1.1.3 Summary

These competition issues in tourism demonstrate that international tourism is a major vehicle for economic development in the twenty-first century. Businesses in the tourism industry in all tourism-based countries need to be sufficiently competitive to share the benefits of increasing globalization. In other words, each business should exploit its own advantages to develop an attractive tourist image based on the specific characteristics of the area in which it operates (including national, local and regional characteristics).

---

flows......the movement of people (labor) and knowledge (technology) across international borders (IMF, 2000)." Internationalization is the process to handle the accumulation of strategies, intangible assets, experiential knowledge, learning, and capabilities across foreign markets (London & Hart, 2004; Rugman & Verbeke, 2004).

Internationalization is sometimes used interchangeably with globalization to refer to economic and cultural effects of an increasingly interconnected world. However, globalization is preferred to the process whereby something (such as a corporation, idea, highway, war and so on) comes to affect multiple nations.

In this dissertation, the author would like to employ globalization to interpret the tourism industry competition under WTO structure.

1.2 Motivation

As introduced above, members of the tourism industry in all tourism-based countries have to understand how to measure and achieve competition, thus improving their competitive edge.

1.2.1 Perspectives on Competitiveness

"Competitiveness" has become a popular term during the past two decades. The meaning, scope, measurement and relevance of competitiveness has been widely discussed in various disciplines, such as economics, management and political science. In terms of international trade theories, competitiveness is defined as "the degree to which a nation can, under free and fair market conditions, produce goods and services that meet the test of international markets, while simultaneously maintaining or expanding the real incomes of its citizens" (Report of the President's Commission on Industrial Competitiveness, 1985). Competitiveness is widely considered as an important factor in creating national prosperity (Durand, Madaschi & Terribile, 1998; The Economist, 1994; European Commission, 1994; Fagerberg, 1988; Fajnzylber, 1988; His Majesty's Treasury, 1983; Krugman, 1994; Newall, 1992; OECD, 2000; Scott & Lodge, 1985), since it improves the standard of living and real income by offering goods and services with some comparative advantages (Crouch & Ritchie, 1999).

However, the increasing growth of international trade means that the increase in trade among countries with similar factorial portfolios is more interesting than trade pattern determination. Michael Porter (1980, 1985 and 1990) proposed a series of new analytic frameworks for measuring competitive advantage, thus achieving a breakthrough in international trade theory. His system was referred as "…a redefinition of the boundaries of strategic management, and a lowering of the barriers which separate strategic management from economics" (Grant, 1991, p. 548). Porter's frameworks are composed of the "five structural forces" model and the diamond model. These models explain the competitiveness of businesses in terms of three main building blocks, namely global competitive environment, competitive strategy and organizational structure. Porter's frameworks can easily be adopted to create insight into how competitiveness is created and sustained (Sim, Ong & Agarwal, 2003).

Porter's frameworks not only lack not only theoretical originality (Dunning, 1993; Greenaway, 1993; Rugman & D'Cruz, 1993), but also predicted the competitiveness of each individual industry poorly (Meliàn-Gonzàlez & Garcia- Falcòn, 2003). Nonetheless, they have become paradigm for competitiveness analysis, and have been widely researched empirically in many fields during the recent 2 decades. (Bess, 2006; Cho, 1994; Cho & Moon, 1998; Dwyer et al., 2000; Enright & Newton, 2004; Fagerberg, 1988; Guan, Yam, Mok & Ma, 2006; Ivanova, Arcelus & Srinivasa, 1998; Kim & Marion, 1997; Moon, Rugman & Verbeke, 1998; Solleiro & Castañón, 2005; Xepapadeas & de Zeeuw, 1999; Zanakis & Becerra-Fernandez, 2005).

The concepts and analysis approaches on competitiveness reveal two principal evolutionary tendencies, namely the Ricardian Comparative Advantages (RCA) theory and Porterian Competitive Advantages (PCA) framework. The RCA theory measures trends in industrial development in a country based on its natural resources. Therefore, RCA views competitiveness at an international level, and can be considered as a long-turn (static) guideline in setting industrial development policy. In contrast, PCA explores the factors that enable a specific industry to succeed in a global competitive environment. Hence, competitiveness on PCA at the global level could be treated as a short-turn (dynamic) tactic in business strategy planning.

To focus on the principal issue of information management, in this study, the composition of tourism competitiveness is so-called tourism competitive information.

1.2.2 Competitiveness Evaluations

Competitiveness in a specific industry results from convergences of the management practices, organizational modes in its country, and the sources of competitive advantage in the industry (Oral, 1986). Therefore, competitiveness in an industry in a country is influenced by a range of qualitative and quantitative factors. Artto (1987), based on the economic theories, indicated that competitiveness can be evaluated from financial status and relative total costs (including cost, price and non-price factors). Traditional cost-benefit analysis (Oral, 1986, 1993; Oral & Reisman, 1988; Li, 2000) is a parametric approach based on optimization technology and regression models. Earlier studies focused mainly on financial indicators, particularly at the firm level. They provided lists of factors that improved competitiveness, but did not explain how these factors were obtained, or the technical assumptions of regression models about the error terms. Resource-based models (Barney, 1991; Peteraf, 1993; Prahalad & Hamel, 1990; Wernerfelt, 1984), with organization management, manufacturing, marketing, and environment as dimensions, have recently been employed to investigate competitiveness.

However, the main factor affecting competitiveness is a controversial issue. In particularly, a single performance criterion (financial profitability) is insufficient for determining the competitiveness of an industry. Consequently, multifactor model is developed to evaluate competitiveness (Chakravarthy, 1986; Chin, Pun & Lau, 2003) by ranking the market competitive positions. Those models provide appropriate strategic combinations to sustain a strong and reasonable competitive edge.

Rapid globalization has led to countries being ranked for competitiveness. The World Economic Forum (WEF, 2005) and the International Institute of Management Development (IMD, 2005) both rate countries annually in terms of various competitiveness indicators. The rankings cause confusion, since they are not based on a rigorous theoretical methodology (the selection factors are not fully explained) or measurement model (no suitable weights are employed to determine the competitiveness indicator of each factor). Additionaly, these two competitiveness reports frequently have significant discrepancies in ranking (Cho & Moon, 2000). Therefore, the ranking system for competitiveness evaluation needs to be redesigned.

1.2.3 Summary

Tourism competitiveness can be defined as, "The relative competitive position (in terms of profits and growth) of a nation's tourism industry in the global market, including developed and developing countries, which could therefore increase the real income of its citizens and improve its standard of living."

The modern concept of competitiveness has evolved from RCA to PCA. Many competitive information evaluations are currently available (including cost-benefit analysis, resource-based points, and ranking reports from WEF to IMD). However, no consensus or systematic analytical structure is available to address how competitiveness should be evaluated. Therefore, these competitiveness evaluations could not accurately indicate how to rectify and improve inefficiencies.

Researchers in tourism research have generally assumed that the measures can accurately capture "truth" (Ritchie, 1975). To address this issue, this dissertation aims to construct suitable competitive indicators to provide consistent comparisons between countries and between industries of the tourism sector. These evaluative indicators should enable countries to identify where their tourism competitiveness may be weaker than others, and recommend appropriate improvements and rectifications.

1.3 Problem Statement

This study has two contributions. Firstly, this study tracks the theoretical evolutions of competitiveness, namely definitions, evaluations and major defects. Second, the scope of tourism competitiveness is defined in order to propose a research framework.

1.3.1 Evolution of Competitiveness

Competitiveness has been widely researched since the international trade revolution derived from Adam Smith's seminal publication, *The Wealth of Nations*, in 1776. However, the differences between RCA and PCA, both in terms of theoretical framework and analytical factors, deserve consideration. This is because the economical environment has changed, since the time of Adam Smith, from very simple international trade situations to today's very complicated global economy. Consequently, the analytical framework of RCA cannot be adapted to modern economic conditions. The evolution of competitiveness from Smith to Porter needs to be well comprehensively understood (Fig. 1.1).

Adam Smith originally proposed that the wealth of nations is created by division of labor and specialization, thus achieving production effectiveness (for each product), i.e., acquiring absolute advantages. However, Ricardo (1817) believed that each country, should determine appropriate products in which to specialize when competing in the world economy, based on its natural resources. These resources cannot be changed. In contrast, a country could acquire other competitive advantages through productivity growth, which could be accomplished through technological change channels. Competitive advantage can be achieved through specialization processes, including physical capital investment, to achieve economies of scale (Dixit & Stiglitz, 1977; Krugman, 1979; Lancaster, 1980), or through human capital investment to achieve knowledge accumulation (Arrow, 1962; Lucas, 1988; Yang, 1994; Yang & Zhang, 2000). This approach is called "**learning by doing**". Another way of achieving competitive advantage is through "**technology innovation**" (Freeman, 1994; Romer, 1990; Schumpeter, 1912). Technological change is often considered as an endogenous variable in an economic growth model (Arrow, 1962; Freeman, 1994; Krugman, 1979; Lucas, 1988; Romer, 1990). Hence, RCA could be divided into exogenous and endogenous comparative advantages, which are respectively based on endowments and technological change.

Economists started to argue in 1994 that traditional trade theories should address other dimensions of competitiveness, instead of productivity itself.

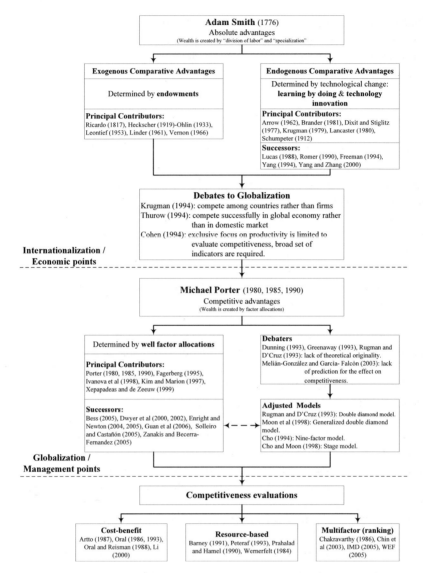

Fig. 1.1 Research framework of competitiveness evolutions

They began to accept Porter's argument that any firm will fail unless it ensures good allocations of resources in the global economy. However, although various models based on Porter's arguments have been proposed, PCA is still a classic methodology for planning development strategies in firm-level, industry-level, and government-level operational management.

Finally, an appropriate methodology can be employed to evaluate tourism competitiveness by reviewing existing methodologies in measuring competitiveness, including cost-benefit analysis, resource-based points, and multifactor (ranking) model.

1.3.2 Composition of Tourism Competitiveness

Since a tourist needs to travel to a destination to experience the destination service, the fundamental product in tourism is the destination experience. Competition focuses on the tourism destination. Although competition occurs among airlines, hotels, facilitates and other tourism services, this inter-industry competition is dependent upon and derived from the choices made by tourists between alternative destinations. Consequently, countries, cities and regions now take their roles as tourist destinations very seriously, and expend considerable effort and funds towards improving their touristic image and attractiveness. Meanwhile, tourism researchers devote their attention to improving the competitiveness of tourism destinations. (Chon & Mayer, 1995; Crouch & Ritchie, 1999, 2000; d'Hauteserre, 2000; Dwyer et al., 2000, 2002; Enright & Newton, 2004, 2005; Faulkner, Oppermann & Fredline, 1999; Hassan, 2000; Hou, Lin & Morais, 2005; Pearce, 1997; Poon, 1993). For example, Pearce (1997, p. 24) indicated that "when tourism worldwide is becoming increasingly competitive... all insights into the development, strengths and weaknesses of competing destinations will become more crucial." Crouch and Ritchie (2000, p. 6) concluded that tourism destination competitiveness "has tremendous ramifications for the tourism industry, and is therefore of considerable interest to practitioners and policy makers." Moreover, Enright and Newton (2005, p. 340) stated that "a destination is competitive if it can attract and satisfy potential tourists, and this competitiveness is determined by both tourism-specific factors and a much wider range of factors that influence the tourism service providers."

Therefore, much of this escalating competitive effort has centered on destination promotion and the tandem role of destination development. However, a destination's competitiveness involves a wide and complex range of issues. Mainstream research into tourism competitiveness have traditionally concentrated on destination image or attractiveness, which refers to attributes that visoitors consider as important (Bonn, Joseph & Dai, 2005; Gallarza, Saura & García, 2002; Gearing, Swart & Var, 1974; Hou et al., 2005; Hsu, Wolfe & Kang, 2004; Hu & Ritchie, 1993). Attractive attributes for tourism destinations include natural resources (e.g., climate, scenery, landscape and minerals), cultural/heritage resources (e.g., history, music, paintings, folklore, temple sites and special events) and functional/ physical resources (e.g., accommodations, food, transportation, guiding services and environmental management). Generally, while tourism services had been viewed as important elements of destination image, explicit attention would be paid to the firms that supply the services, and to the factors that may influence the competitiveness of these firms. In other words, the main issue is company management rather than destination competitiveness (Buhails, 2000). However, Murphy, Pritchard and Smith (2000) concluded that both environment conditions and infrastructure have a strong bearing on tourists' perceptions, which in turn influence their assessment of a destination's competitiveness. Therefore, to understand the competitiveness of tourism destinations, Crouch and Ritchie (1999) presented an approach to destination attractiveness analysis that is more comprehensive than mainstream approaches. Their approach considers both the fundamental elements and advanced elements of competitive advantages. Appropriate, prompt tourism management activities could not only enhance the attractiveness of those comparative advantages and competitive advantages, but also adapt to the constraints imposed by the domestic and global environment, such as resources stewardship, marketing activities, regulation, business integration and information providing (Enright & Newton, 2004, 2005).

This study defines tourism competitiveness as the ability of a destination to create, integrate and deliver tourism experiences, including value-added goods and services considered to be important by tourists. These experiences sustain the resources of a destination, and help it maintain a good market position relative to other destinations. This study of tourism competitiveness is based on a competitiveness evolutions framework (Fig. 1.1), and is composed of comparative advantages, competitive advantages and tourism management (as Fig. 1.2).

1.4 Contributions

This study investigates the competitiveness of the tourism industry. This study also proposes a framework for ranking countries by with competitiveness. The proposed framework is composed of a measuring model and competitiveness indicators. Moreover, can improve operation efficiency, and manage each country's economic strengths and weaknesses in terms of tourism resources. Countries can thus compete effectively in the international market, or cooperate with each other to enhance overall competitiveness, thus becoming more attractive in the international market.

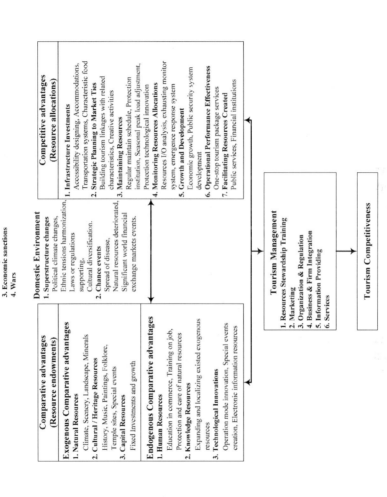

Fig. 1.2 Research framework of tourism competitive information

After presenting briefly the background, motivation and purpose of this research in Chap. 1, Chap. 2 presents an exhaustive related literature review to identify a theoretical evolutions context of global competitiveness from trade theory (RCA) to competitiveness theory (PCA). Chapter 2 also reviews relevant literature for competitiveness evaluation and measurement indicators.

Chapter 3 describes the related methodology of implementing tourism global competitiveness evaluation, based on the consistent concepts and scopes presented in Chap. 2. No consensus exists around the factors involved in measuring competitiveness. Additionally, competitiveness evaluation, particularly in the tourism industry, requires a systematic analytical structure. Therefore, adaptive evaluation indicators of competitiveness in tourism industry are selected according to related literature. These indicators are then employed to construct the competitiveness evaluation model of the tourism industry. Additionally, the evaluation methodology and procedure are determined under feasible implementation considerations. The proposed competitiveness evaluation model will hopefully provide metrics for comparing the economic strengths and weaknesses of each country's tourism industry The model should therefore improve cooperation between countries to enhance their overall global competitiveness.

Chapter 4 extends determines the weight of each factor in the evaluation model constructed in Chap. 3. The AHP questionnaire survey, clearly aims to obtain an overall picture, in order to understand the importance of each factor. It can thus theoretically determine the priority for improving each factor.

Finally, Chap. 5 presents the analysis of interaction effects between RCA and PCA. This analysis provides the primary implications for allocation of tourism resources. Some useful policy suggestions are also discussed.

References

Adam S (1776) An inquiry into the nature and causes of the wealth of nations (Modern Library). Random House: New York.

APEC Tourism Charter (2000) Seoul Declaration on APEC Tourism Charter. The 1st APEC tourism ministerial meeting. APEC Tourism Charter: Seoul.

Archer B (1987) Demand forecasting and estimation. In: Ritchie J, Goeldner C (eds) Travel, tourism and hospitality research. New York: Wiley.

Arrow KJ (1962) The economic implications of learning by doing. The Review of Economic Studies 29:155–173.

Artto EW (1987) Relative total costs—An approach to competitiveness measurement of industries. Management International Review 27:47–58.

Barney JB (1991) Firm resources and sustainable competitive advantages. Journal of Management 17:99–120.

Bess R (2006) New Zealand seafood firm competitiveness in export markets: The role of the quota management system and aquaculture legislation. Marine Policy 30:367–378.

Bonn MA, Joseph SM, Dai M (2005) International versus domestic visitors: An examination of destination image perceptions. Journal of Travel Research 43:294–301.

Brander JA (1981) Intra-industry trade in identical commodities. Journal of International Economics 11:1–14.

Buhails D (2000) Marketing the competitive destination of the future. Tourism Management 21:97–116.

Chakravarthy BS (1986) Measuring strategic performance. Strategic Management Journal 7:437–458.

Chin KS, Pun KF, Lau H (2003) Development of a knowledge-based self-assessment system for measuring organizational performance. Expert Systems with Application 24:443–455.

Cho DS (1994) A dynamic approach to international competitiveness: The case of Korea. Journal of Far Eastern Business 1:17–36.

Cho DS, Moon HC (1998) A nation's international competitiveness in different stages of economic development. Advances in Competitiveness Research 6: 5–19.

Cho DS, Moon HC (2000) From Adam Smith to Michael Porter: Evolution of competitiveness theory. World Scientific Publishing Co: Singapore.

Chon KS, Mayer KJ (1995) Destination competitiveness models in tourism and their application in Las Vegas. Journal of Tourism Systems and Quality Management 1:227–246.

Cohen SS (1994) Speaking freely. Foreign Affairs 73:194–197.

Crouch GI, Ritchie JRB (1999) Tourism, competitiveness, and societal prosperity. Journal of Business Research 44:137–152.

Crouch GI, Ritchie JRB (2000) The competitive destination: A sustainability perspective. Tourism Management 21:1–7.

Dharmaratne GS (1995) Forecasting tourist arrivals in Barbados. Annals of Tourism Research 22:804–818.

d'Hauteserre AM (2000) Lessons in managed destination competitiveness: The case of Foxwoods Casino Resort. Tourism Management 21:23–32.

Dixit AK, Stiglitz JE (1977) Monopolistic competition and optimum product diversity. The American Economic Review 67:297–308.

Dunning JH (1993) Internationalizing Porter's diamond. Management International Review 33:7–15.

Durand M, Madaschi C, Terribile F (1998) Trends in OECD countries' international competitiveness: The influence of emerging market economies. Economics Department Working Papers No. 195, OECD, Paris.

Dwyer L, Forsyth P, Rao P (2000) The price competitiveness of travel and tourism: A comparison of 19 destinations. Tourism Management 21:9–22.

Dwyer L, Forsyth P, Rao P (2002) Destination price competitiveness: Exchange rate changes versus domestic inflation. Journal of Travel Research 40: 328–336.

Enright MJ, Newton J (2004) Tourism destination competitiveness: A quantitative approach. Tourism Management 25:777–788.

Enright MJ, Newton J (2005) Determinants of tourism destination competitiveness in Asia Pacific: Comprehensiveness and universality. Journal of Travel Research 43:339–350.

European Commission (1994) Competitiveness Advisory Group, Enhancing European Competitiveness, 2nd Report to The President of The Commission, OOPEC, Luxembourg.

Fagerberg J (1988) International competitiveness. The Economic Journal 98: 355–374.

Fagerberg J (1995) User-producer interaction, learning and comparative advantage. Cambridge Journal of Economics 19:243 256.

Fajnzylber F (1988) International competitiveness: Agreed goal, hard task. CEPAL Review 36:7–23.

Faulkner B, Oppermann M, Fredline E (1999) Destination competitiveness: An exploratory examination of South Australia's core attractions. Journal of Vacation Marketing 5:125–139.

Freeman C (1994) The economics of technical change. Cambridge Journal of Economics 18:463–514.

Gallarza MG, Saura IG, García HC (2002) Destination image: Towards a Conceptual Framework. Annals of Tourism Research 29:56–72.

Gearing CE, Swart WW, Var T (1974) Establishing a measure of touristic attractiveness. Journal of Travel Research 12:1–8.

Greenaway D (1993) The competitive advantage of nations by Michael E. Porter. Kyklos 46:145–146.

Grant RM (1991) Porter's competitive advantage of nations: An assessment. Strategic Management Journal 12:535–548.

Guan JC, Yam RCM, Mok CK et al. (2006) A study of the relationship between competitiveness and technological innovation capability based on DEA models. European Journal of Operational Research 170:971–986.

Hassan SS (2000) Determinants of market competitiveness in an environmentally sustainable tourism industry. Journal of Travel Research 38:239–245

Heckscher E (1919) The effect of foreign trade on the distribution of income. Economisk Tidskrift, 21:497–512.

His Majesty's Treasury (1983) International competitiveness. Economic Progress Report 158:1– 5.

Hou JS, Lin CH, Morais DB (2005) Antecedents of attachment to a cultural tourism destination: The case of Hakka and non-Hakka Taiwanese visitors to Pei-pu, Taiwan. Journal of Travel Research 44:221–233.

Hsu CHC, Wolfe K, Kang SK (2004) Image assessment for a destination with limited comparative advantages. Tourism Management 25:121–126.

Hu YZ, Ritchie JRB (1993) Measuring destination attractiveness: A contextual approach. Journal of Travel Research 32:25–34.

International Monetary Fund (IMF) (2000) Globalization: Threat or opportunity? IMF: Washington DC.

International Institute for Management Development (IMD) (2005) The World competitiveness yearbook 2005. Lausanne: Switzerland.

Ivanova IM, Arcelus FJ, Srinivasan G (1998) Assessment of the competitiveness position of the Latin American countries. International Journal of Commerce & Management 8:7–32.

Kim D, Marion BW (1997) Domestic market structure and performance in global markets: theory and empirical evidence from U.S. food manufacturing industries. Review of Industrial Organization 12:335–354.

Krugman P (1979) Increasing returns, monopolistic competition and international trade. Journal of International Economics 9:469–479.

Krugman P (1994) Competitiveness: A dangerous obsession. Foreign Affairs 73:28–46.

Lancaster KJ (1980) Intra-industry trade under perfect monopolistic competition. Journal of International Economics 10:151–175.

Leontief W (1953) Domestic production and foreign trade: The American capital position re-examined. Proceedings of the American Philosophical Society 97:332–349.

Li LX (2000) An analysis of sources of competitiveness and performance of Chinese manufacturers. International Journal of Operations & Production Management 20:299–315.

Linder SB (1961) An essay on trade and transformation. John Wiley: New York.

London T, Hart SL (2004) Reinventing strategies for emerging markets: beyond the transnational model. Journal of International Business Studies 35:350–371.

Lucas RE (1988) On the mechanism of economic development. Journal of Monetary Economics 22:3–42.

Meliàn-Gonzàlez A, Garcia-Falcòn JM (2003) Competitive potential of tourism in destinations. Annals of Tourism Research 30:720–740.

Moon HC, Rugman AM, Verbeke A (1998) A generalized double diamond approach to the international competitiveness of Korea and Singapore. International Business Review 7:135–150.

Murphy P, Pritchard MP, Smith B (2000) The destination product and its impact on traveler perceptions. Tourism Management 21:43–52.

Newall JE (1992) The challenge of competitiveness. The Business Quarterly 56:94–100.

OECD (2000) The competitiveness of European industry: 1999 Report. Working Document of The Services of The European Commission: COM(1999) 465. OECD, Paris.

Ohlin B (1933) Interregional and international trade. Harvard University Press: Cambridge.

Oral M (1986) An industrial competitiveness model. IIE Transactions 18:148–157.

Oral M (1993) A methodology for competitiveness analysis and strategy formulation in glass industry. European Journal of Operational Research 68:9–22.

Oral M, Reisman A (1988) Measuring industrial competitiveness. Industrial Marketing Management 17:263–272.

Pai PF, Hong WC (2005) An improved neural network model in forecasting arrivals. Annals of Tourism Research 32:1138–1141.

Patsouratis V, Frangouli Z, Anastasopoulos G (2005) Competition in tourism among the Mediterranean countries. Applied Economics 37:1865–1880.

Pearce DG (1997) Competitive destination analysis in Southeast Asia. Journal of Travel Research 36:16–24.

Peteraf MA (1993) The cornerstones of competitive advantages: A resource-based view. Strategic Management Journal 14:179–191.

Poon A (1993) Tourism, technology and competitive strategy. CAB International: Wallingford (UK).

Porter ME (1980) Competitive strategy: Techniques for analyzing industries and competitors. The Free Press: New York.

Porter ME (1985) Competitive advantages: Creating and sustaining superior performance. The Free Press: New York.

Porter ME (1990) The competitive advantages of nations. The Free Press: New York.

Prahalad CK, Hamel G (1990) The core competence of the corporation. Harvard Business Review 68:79–91.

Report of the President's Commission on Industrial Competitiveness (1985) Global competition: The new reality. U.S. Government Printing Office: Washington DC.

Ricardo D (1971/1817) On the principles of political economy and taxation. Penguin: Baltimore.

Ritchie JRB (1975) Some critical aspects of measurement theory and practice in travel research. Journal of Travel Research 14:1–10.

Ritchie JRB, Crouch GI (2000) The competitive destination: A sustainability perspective. Tourism Management 21:1–7.

Romer P (1990) Endogenous technological change. Journal of Political Economy 98:S71–S102.

Rugman AM, D'Cruz JR (1993) The double diamond model of international competitiveness: The Canadian experiences. Management International Review 33:17–39.

Rugman AM, Verbeke A (2004) A perspective on regional and global strategies of multinational enterprises. Journal of International Business Studies 35:3–19.

Schumpeter J (1912) The theory of economic development. Duncker & Humblot: Leipzig. Reprinted in 1934 by Cambridge: Harvard University Press, and added subtitle "An inquiry into profits, capital, interest and the business cycle."

Scott BR, Lodge GC (1985) U.S. competitiveness in the World economy. Harvard Business School Press: Boston M A.

Sim LL, Ong SE, Agarwal A (2003) Singapore's competitiveness as a global city: Development strategy, institutions and business environment. Cities 20: 115–127.

Solleiro JL, Castañón R (2005) Competitiveness and innovation systems: The challenges for Mexico's insertion in the global context. Technovation 25:1059–1070.

The Economist (1994) The economics of meaning. The Economist, April 30, 331(7861): 17–18.

Thurow LC (1994) Microchips, not potato chips. Foreign Affairs 73:189–192.

United Nations World Tourism Organization (UNWTO) (2005) Tourism highlights 2005. UNWTO, Madrid, Spain.

Vernon R (1966) International investments and international trade in the product cycle. Quarterly Journal of Economics 81:190–207.

Wernerfelt B (1984) A resource-based view of the firm. Strategic Management Journal 5:171–180.

World Economic Forum (WEF) (2005) The global competitiveness report 2005. WEF: Switzerland.

World Travel and Tourism Council (WTTC) (2005) Progress and priorities 2005–06. WTTC: UK.

Xepapadeas A, de Zeeuw A (1999) Environmental policy and competitiveness: The Porter hypothesis and the composition of capital. Journal of Environmental Economics and Management 37:165–182.

Yang XK (1994) Endogenous vs. exogenous comparative advantage and economies of specialization vs. economies of scale. Journal of Economics 60:29–54.

Yang XK, Zhang DS (2000) Endogenous structure of the division of labor, endogenous trade policy regime, and a dual structure in economic development. Annals of Economics and Finance 1:211–230.

Zanakis SH, Becerra-Fernandez I (2005) Competitiveness of nations: A knowledge discovery examination. European Journal of Operational Research 166:185–211.

2 Literature Reviews

Until the late 1980s, a theoretical framework for analyzing, maintaining and improving the evolution of national or industrial competitiveness described in Chap. 1 (Fig. 1.1) has been unavailable. However, similar economic analyses of competitiveness have been performed using different measures and terms. For example, Classic Economics (Smith, 1776; Ricardo, 1817) evaluated the property of a country (i.e., national competitiveness) by its factor endowments; the Austrian School of Economics (Schumpeter, 1912) claimed that competitiveness is acquired via innovation approaches; List (1837), a pioneer in the German Historical School, indicated that "productive powers" enables an economy to achieve competitiveness; Institutional Economics proposed that economic systems and institutions of a country shape its corresponding competitiveness. Therefore, a review of the relevant economic literature is needed to understand the theoretical background of global competitiveness.

However, of these seminal works in economic theory, a suitable perspective and core framework is needed to understand the evolution of competitiveness. This study examines the research framework of industrial global competitiveness by reviewing the evolution of international trade theory. Because international trade is the primary economic relationship between countries, international trade relationships are representative of industrial global competition. On the other hand, theories of international trade involve value, distribution and resource allocations between trading partners, therefore, "each possible approach to general economic theory has its corresponding theory of trade and any changes or developments in general theory must have implications for the theory of international trade (Eatwell et al., 1991, Vol. 2, p. 406)".

The Ricardian and Porterian views are the two major theoretical frameworks for analyzing global competition. The RCA was first proposed by David Ricardo in 1817. The theory argues that even countries or regions which are not the most efficient commodity producers can still participate in and benefit from international trade (Baron & Kemp, 2004; Davis & Weinstein, 2003; Fisher & Kakkar, 2004). This theory held sway in global competition analysis for over a century. As John Maynard Keynes said, "the principle of survival of the fittest can be regarded as a vast generalization of

W.-C. Hong, *Competitiveness in the Tourism Sector.* Contributions to Economics,
doi: 10.1007/978-3-7908-2042-3_2, © Physica-Verlag Heidelberg 2008

Ricardian economics".[1] Porterian competitive analysis (Porter, 1980, 1985 & 1990) proposes a model of five structural forces and a diamond model, which included three main building blocks, namely, global competitive environment, competitive strategy and organizational structure to explain the competitiveness of businesses (firms). These theories provide insight into the creation and sustenance of international industrial competitiveness. (Sim et al., 2003).

The following is an overview of the literature regarding exogenous comparative advantage, endogenous comparative advantage, competitive advantage and proposed indicators for evaluating economic competitiveness.

2.1 Exogenous Comparative Advantage Theory

Comparative advantage theories can be classified according to the manner in which the advantage is acquired. Exogenous comparative advantage is one such international trade theory, and is based on analysis of the comparative endowment of natural resources among trading partners. Representative theories are those of Ricardo (1817), Heckscher (1919), Ohlin (1933), Leontief (1953), Linder (1961), and Vernon (1966).

2.1.1 Enlightenment of Adam Smith's Absolute Advantage

Adam Smith (1776) viewed trade as a positive-sum game in which all partners can benefit. Smith indicated that each partner, based on its natural endowments, should concentrate on what it can do better than others, i.e., via "division of labor" and "specialization" to acquire an advantage in natural endowments, namely, absolute advantage. Smith suggested that division of labor and specialization enable a country to enhance its productivity. Additionally, the "invisible hand" theory of Smith indicated that market competition leads each person and each country to do what they are best suitable to provide their maximum services and contribution to their products. In The Wealth of Nations, Smith modernized international economic theory and firmly established the importance of the Ricardo theory of comparative advantage.

---

[1] Quoted in Skidelsky (1992, p. 225).

2.1.2 Introduction and Discussion

2.1.2.1 Basic Concepts

However, the applicability of absolute advantage theory was questioned in the case of a country with absolute advantage in all goods. According to the Smith model, such a dominant country would not benefit from international trade. On the other hand, Ricardo argued that the model was still applicable. Trade between a dominant country and a country with no absolute advantage can still benefit both countries. This model is the well-known "Ricardo comparative advantage (RCA)" theory. According to Ricardo, labor is a unique production factor, and productivity (technology) differences between countries become the basis of comparison. However, Ricardo did not explain the cause of these differences, i.e., why technology levels should be viewed as exogenous endowments.

In the 1920s two Swedish economists, Eli Heckscher (1919) and his student Bertil Ohlin (1933) proposed an important new international trade theory now known as the Heckscher-Ohlin model. This model proposed that differences in factor endowments determine production cost, which then produce comparative advantages. A country should export those commodities that they possess in relative abundance and import those that are relatively scarce. In addition, in the H-O model, the technology is similar, but production methods differ between countries, where different production methods imply different combinations of capital and labor.

2.1.2.2 Debates and Discussions

In 1953, Wassily Leontief implemented the most influential empirical study of trade patterns based on H-O theory. Leontief surprisingly calculated that, in 1947, the capital per man required to produce a $1 million of exports was less than the capital per man required to produced a $1 million of import substitutes (approximately 30%). The implication at that time was that the U.S. was exporting labor-intensive commodities and importing more capital-intensive commodities. This finding, known as the Leontief Paradox, was the opposite of what the H-O theory.

In the 1960s, Staffan Linder (1961) proposed the country similarity theory to explain international trade among countries with similar characteristics. Linder argued that countries with similar income levels have similar consumption preferences.

Raymond Vernon (1966) argued that comparative advantages in commodities shift over time from one country to another via his famous product cycle theory (PCT) of introduction, growth, maturity, and decline. The PCT employed a dynamic analytical approach to describing shifts in international division of labor and the transfers of international trade patterns. Particularly, PCT satisfactorily reconciles the Leontief paradox that the U.S. exports products in the introduction stage when production is labor-intensive and imports products in the mature stage when production is capital-intensive.

2.1.3 Summary

As mentioned above, the concept of exogenous comparative advantage provides several useful theoretical points for analysis of industrial global competitiveness: firstly, the lower production cost is, the superior its global competitiveness, therefore, countries should develop industries with relatively lower production costs. Secondly, production cost in a specific industry depends on its factor endowments; therefore, countries should develop industries with relatively abundant factors. Although some of the examined theories may lack explanatory power, and succeeding theories based on assumptions of complete competition and constant returns to scale only partially addressed the inadequacies of the H-O model, these theories are still applicable. They still provide different perspectives for clarifying how international trade policies and global competitiveness are maintained.

2.2 Endogenous Comparative Advantage Theory

The rapid growth and structural changes in international trade among the industrial countries during the postwar period to the late 1970s prompted western economists to analyze the problems of increasing return to scale (economies of scale) and imperfect competition. Analytical models were needed to explain international trade problems such as motivation to trade, international specialization and trade policy making. In contrast with the Ricardian view, neo-trade theoreticians further elaborated on the Schumpeter (1912) theory of innovation processes and the Arrow (1962) theory of learning by doing. Neo-trade theoreticians concluded that comparative advantages could be acquired along with productivity growth and that productivity growth could be achieved via technological change channels. One such change was is specialization, including physical capital investment to achieve economies of scale (Dixit & Stiglitz, 1977; Krugman, 1979; Lancaster, 1980) and human capital investment to achieve knowledge accumulation (Lucas, 1988; Yang, 1994; Yang & Zhang, 2000), namely, learning by doing. Another change is technology innovation

(Romer, 1990; Freeman, 1994). Because technology is not an endowment in any country, technological change is often viewed as an endogenous variable in economic growth models.

2.2.1 Specialization Processes

2.2.1.1 Economies of Scale (Physical Capital Investment)

In their studies of monopolistic competition and optimum product diversity, Dixit and Stiglitz (1977) argued that, due to economies of scale, resources can be saved and countries (firms) can benefit by elasticity of utility, that is, producing fewer commodities in larger quantities. Based on their findings, Krugman (1979) developed a general equilibrium model of Chamberlinian monopolistic competition which indicated that trade is driven by economies of scale instead of different factor endowments or technology. The Krugman model is still applied by industrial economists to analyze the economic effects of geography and home market in location decision making (Davis & Weinstein, 2003). Further, Lancaster (1980) showed that, in the Chamberlinian model of monopolistic competition, if the effects of factor intensities in production (H-O model) are small relative to the effects of economies of scale for individual products (particularly for intra-industry, such as large cars and small cars), countries may specialize in products with scale economies rather than trade products based on the H-O model.

As briefly mentioned above, since the late 1970s, economies of scale have become the most important research issue in international trade theories. In acquiring the economies of scale, physical capital investment by a firm or country is the key to succeed. The successors had theoretically divided economies of scale into three different forms: (1) *Internal economies of scale*. In a firm, larger scales of production reduce average costs due to economies of scale in technical, managerial, financial, marketing, commercial and research and development. (2) *External economies of scale*. At the industry level rather than at the individual firm level, a cluster of small firms in a specific geographic area may make each individual firm more efficient. The development of specialized suppliers, labor market pooling and knowledge spillover can reduce manufacturing costs in an industry and produce a competitive advantage for a geographic area. (3) *Dynamic economies of scale*. In an infant industry with dynamically increasing returns, production costs fall due to cumulative production experience over time rather than increased rate of production, i.e., producers learn by doing. Producers can release a new product and get a jump on the competition in movement along the "learning curve." Therefore, dynamic economies of scale often justify protectionism to temporarily protect industries while producers gain experience.

2.2.1.2 Learning by Doing (Human Capital Investment)

"Learning by doing", also known as human capital investment to accumulate knowledge, is another approach in the specialization processes. In the 1960s, Arrow (1962) proposed viewing knowledge as an endogenous variable of economic growth underlying intertemporal and international shifts in production function. Efficiently acquiring and accumulating knowledge is the engine of economic growth. However, learning is the product of experience, and learning can only occur through the attempt to solve a problem or during activity (production). Steadily increasing performance (experiences) requires steadily evolving rather than merely repeating, namely, labor productivity progress, also known as "progress ratio" or "learning curve" (Hirsch, 1956). Further, Lucas (1988) proposed that learning by doing in any particular activity occurs rapidly at first, then more slowly, then not at all. However, if trade in new commodities is introduced into the world economy (i.e. free trade), particularly when labor has mobility, these technologies cause spillover from one person to another via export of these commodities or the movement of labor. Therefore, human capital growth can be enhanced by the meticulous processes of learning-by-doing.

In contrast with Arrow (1962) and Lucas (1988), Yang (1994) and colleagues (Yang & Zhang, 2000) analyzed the economies of division of labor (i.e. economies of specialization) and transaction cost theory in their proposal that endogenous comparative advantages are acquired by specializing to accumulate human capital and knowledge. They indicated that, along with the specialization processes, transaction costs and other costs necessary for executing transactions, such as transaction technology, institutional arrangements and learning (specializing in a single commodity), increase concurrently. Under this cost constraint condition, any country can determine the suitable level of individual specialization, which Yang (1994) and Yang and Zhang (2000) termed "transaction efficiency", enabling the division of labor to improve repeatedly until economies of specialization are achieved.

This concept of specialization according to comparative advantage, even though larger countries may not be completely specialized, is still viewed as the unique evolutionarily stable state of the world economy (Fisher & Kakkar, 2004).

2.2.2 Technological Innovation

Another approach to technological change is technology innovation, which results from investment and R&D (research and development). In the early 1910s, Schumpeter (1912) argued that innovation processes interrupt the "circular flow" of economic life. He explained that technological change caused by innovation causes economic life to go through a number of cyclic fluctuations. Subsequent researchers in technological innovation such as Pavitt (1980) proposed that cumulative advantages in know-how, skills and innovative capability may underlie some of the persistent differences in comparative international trade and productivity performance. Romer (1990) indicated that technological innovation provides the incentive for continued capital accumulation. Freeman (1994) employed the instrument industry and the software industry as examples to demonstrate that large firms are still capable of the great majority of innovations in most industries, and small firms tend to be concentrated in only a few industrial sectors.

Competition in international trade markets stimulates trading partners to conduct R&D in new products and technologies. However, along with international trade activities, technological spillover provides trading partners with valuable opportunities to learn from each other. Therefore, R&D and technological innovation are not only an individual country activity but a collaborative activity involving all partners.

2.2.3 Summary

Analysis of endogenous comparative advantage provides several useful theoretical insights into industrial global competitiveness. Firstly, production cost is not the only determining consideration. Industrial global competitiveness is simultaneously determined by numerous factors including economies of scale, economies of specialization, transaction cost, technological innovation, etc. Secondly, in contrast with the exogenous comparative advantage view, every country should not only develop the industries in which it enjoys relatively abundant factors, but also focus on ex post training in production ability.

In 1994, Krugman (1994) argued that most trade theoreticians, whether Traditional theoretician or Neo-trade theoretician, almost always focus on productivity. Restated, most measure the competitiveness of a country by its ability to produce commodities and services that meet the test of international competition and enable their citizens to enjoy a standard of living that is both rising and sustainable. He proposed that trade should not be considered a zero-sum game and proposed three dangers of competitiveness. Firstly, it could result in the wasteful spending of government money which could otherwise be used to enhance competitiveness. Secondly, it could lead to protectionism and trade wars. Finally, it could result in bad public policy.

In contrast with Krugman, Thurow (1994) performed a case study indicating that 93% of economic success or failure is determined at home, and only 7% depends on competitive and cooperative arrangements with the rest of the world. He then proposed that the rate of productivity growth in any economy is principally determined by domestic investment in plants and equipment, R&D, technology and public infrastructure as well as the quality of private management and public administration. Hence, for a domestic economy to increase productivity, it must first compete successfully in the global economy. Additionally, Thurow emphasized that foreign competition forces economic change and creates opportunities to learn new technologies and management practices which can improve domestic productivity.

Cohen (1994) argued that focusing exclusively on productivity produces an incomplete analysis of competitiveness. Cohen believed that competitiveness puts productivity at the center of its concerns and that overall productivity rates are very complex syntheses that economics does not know how to do that. Therefore, competitiveness should be analyzed by a broader set of indicators, none of which alone tells the complete story but together may yield important insight.

After the debate between Krugman, Thurow and Cohen in 1994, trade theories attempted to adequately explain the trade forces in the complex global economy system of today. Thus, scholars in the management field employed experiential induction to identify predictive factors for success in an age of global competition. The most important contribution was that of Professor Michael Porter. And, this indicated that Porterian Age is coming. According to the Porterian view, any firm unable to effectively arrange factor allocations is unlikely to survive in the global economy.

2.3 Competitive Advantages

2.3.1 Introduction

Beginning in 1980, Professor Michael Porter published a "trilogy" of his research results: *Competitive Strategies* (1980), *Competitive Advantage* (1985), and *The Competitive Advantage of Nations* (1990). The former two works concentrated on essentials of business competition and principles of competition strategies. The subsequent works extended those theoretical propositions to global competition research. Thus, Porter, via a 4-year study of trading nations, proposed the "national diamond model" to explore how nations acquire competitive advantage in particular industries, and stimulus policies and environments.

In the so-called diamond model, Porter indicated that national prosperity is created rather than inherited, particularly well factor allocations. He concluded that each country acquires competitive advantage in a particular industry from the combined effects of the following four broad attributes: factor conditions, demand conditions, related and supporting industries, and firm strategy, structure and rivalry. In the meanwhile, two outside variables, government and chance, are another dimension indicating the government action needed to create/improve the economic development environment of a country, such as economic stimulus policy. The six attributes, according to the Porter model (as Fig. 2.1), simultaneously interact with each other and collectively constitute a dynamic and stimulating competitive environment which eventually establishes the industrial global competitive advantage of a country. A brief introduction of these attributes follows.

1. Factor conditions. This attribute indicates the factors of production necessary for a country to compete in a specific industry, such as infrastructure and abundant and highly qualified labor. Porter grouped these factors into five categories: human resources, physical resources, knowledge resources, capital resources and infrastructure. Furthermore, to understand the enduring role of factors in competitive advantage, Porter considered that nations succeed in industries where they are particularly good at creating and, most importantly, upgrading the needed factors. Henceforth, nations would be competitive due to unusually high quality of *institutional mechanisms* for specialized factor creation. The factor creation mechanisms in a nation are more important to competitive advantage than the current factor possessed by the nation.

2. Demand conditions. This attribute indicates the influence of the products or services of an industry. Three characteristics of home demand are home demand composition; home demand size and pattern of growth; and internationalization of domestic demand.

   (i) Home demand composition. The first element is the segmented structure of home demand. Firms in a country can acquire competitive advantage in global segments that represent a larger or more visible share of home demand than other countries. The second element is sophisticated and demanding buyers. The most

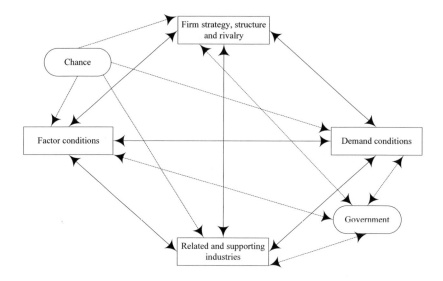

Fig. 2.1 The complete system of national competitiveness
Source: Porter (1990).

sophisticated buyers pressure local firms to innovate faster, both physically and culturally, to create new products or services. The third is anticipatory buyer needs. Home demand provides an earlier indicator of buyer needs than the demand of other countries.

(ii) Home demand size and pattern of growth. Porter argued that the strength of a large home market is due to the existence of economies of scale. Conversely, a large home market may be a weakness limiting local firms from exporting overseas (Switzerland, Sweden, Korea, and Japan are often noted examples).

(iii) Internationalization of domestic demand. This characteristic increases the overseas sales of products and services of a nation; thus, it enhances competitive advantage by employing multinationals to establish overseas markets or by promoting domestic products reflecting local conditions or historical ties.

3. Related and supporting industries. Competitive advantage in some supplier industries provides potential advantages for firms in many other industries of a country because they produce inputs that are important to innovation and internationalization. Supplier industries in a nation create advantages in downstream industries in several ways: via efficient, early and rapid access to the most cost-effective

input or by transmitting information (including new ideas and insights, and suppliers innovations) from firm to firm in the process of innovation and upgrading. On the other hand, an internationally successful industry in a nation provides opportunities for information flow and technical interchange (namely pull-through effect) to increase demand for complementary products or services in related industries.

4. Firm strategy, structure and rivalry. This attribute is the fourth determinant of national competitive advantage in an industry in which firms are created, organized and managed as well as the nature of domestic rivalry. The industries of a nation can acquire competitive advantage only if their management practices and modes of organization are suited to the national environment. Domestic rivalry often creates pressure on firms to improve and innovate to preserve advantages for long periods.

5. Government. The role of this attribute is that of catalyst in shaping the context and institutional structure surrounding companies (e.g. diminishing trade barrier and pricing intervention) and in creating an environment that stimulates companies to acquire competitive advantage (e.g. providing high quality education and training, adequate infrastructure, and public goods; reducing transaction costs, and so on). Additionally, governments should also play a challenger role to encourage or even push firms to raise their aspirations and move to higher levels of performance, even though this process may be difficult.

6. Chance. Events have little to do with circumstances in a nation and are often largely outside the power of firms (and often the national government) to influence. Some examples of particularly influential competitive advantage are the following: pure invention; technological discontinuities; discontinuities in input costs; significant shifts in world financial markets or exchange rates; surge in global or regional demand; political decisions by foreign government; wars. Chance events are important because they create discontinuities that can shift competitive position. Of course, chance events have asymmetric impacts on different nations.

2.3.2 Debates, Adjusted Models, and Successors

2.3.2.1 Debates and Adjusted Models

Since Porter published his book in 1990, the response (including debates) of Western governments, businesses and scholars has been mixed. Many scholars believe Porter bridged the gap between strategic management and international economics. For example, Grant (1991, p. 548) called the text, "...a redefinition of the boundaries of strategic management, and a lowering of the barriers which separate strategic management from economics." Ryan (1990) observed that "the book is meant to be a contemporary equivalent of The Wealth of Nations, and the Free Press is marketing the volume as the new-forged version of Adam Smith's world-transforming thunderbolt." However, most of the criticism was from economists, who questioned the methodology and empirical adjusted models of the work.

1. Methodological Debates and Empirical Works

Greenaway (1993) indicated that PCA requires a more formal analysis. Dunning (1993) analyzed six distinguishing features of the global economy of the 1990s, particularly the cross-border value added activities of multinational enterprises (MNEs), in a reappraisal of the Porter diamond model. Rugman and D'Cruz (1993) argued that "none of these determinants is new or unexpected." Melián-González and García-Falcón (2003) also indicated that the Porter diamond model lacks predictive value in analyzing the effect of competitiveness on each industry.

Hence, many scholars have conducted empirical research to test the Porter model. Fagerberg (1988) analyzed data for 16 OECD countries in 1965, 1973 and 1987 to construct a logarithmic transformation regression model of the international competitiveness of a country. The empirical results indicated that the factor of advanced domestic users positively impacts international competitiveness. Kim and Marion (1997) used the trade performance data of U.S. food manufacturing industries during 1967, 1977 and 1987 as input for establishing a multivariate linear regression model to demonstrate the Porter hypothesis that the degree of competition in a domestic market is positively linked to performance in international markets. Ivanova et al. (1998) applied the Porter framework in constructing a new evaluation model to assess the competitive potential of Latin American countries. The analytical results of the Ivanova study indicated that their proposed model could accurately analyze and forecast international trade trends and assist businesses and governments in making strategic investment decisions. Xepapadeas and Zeeuw (1999) developed a theoretical model to confirm the Porter hypothesis of a win-win situation in which environmental policy improves both environment and competitiveness. These empirical studies were mostly limited to the relationships between industrial competitiveness and some factor or subfactor proposed by Porter.

2. Application Debates and Adjusted Models

Conversely, many scholars have challenged the validity of the Porter model. Some believe the Porter model explains only the success of U.S., Japanese and the UK countries which possess "well" domestic economic environments. However, smaller, less developed and developing countries lack these "well" determinants. Clearly, the Porter model has limited value for explaining the dynamic changes in these countries. Therefore, to address this drawback, several scholars modified the Porter diamond model. For example, Rugman and C'ruz (1993) performed a case study of Canada to revise the Porter model and proposed the "double diamond" model; Moon et al. (1998) extended the applicability of the double diamond model to all small countries with their "generalized double diamond model;" Cho (1994) proposed a nine-factor model based on a Korean case study to provide a more suitable explanation for less developed, developing countries; finally, Cho and Moon (1998) argued that different stages and patterns of economic development influence the decisions of each countries as to which factors to utilize, thus revealing differences in competitiveness status.They therefore suggested a new model for measuring stage of economic development and for further explaining the international competitiveness of a country.

2.3.2.2 Successors

Theoretical models are an abstraction of specific real economic phenomena. It may be impossible to construct a theoretical model that is applicable in all cases. As mentioned above, many models based on different observations of economic phenomena have been proposed. Thus, all proposed models are limited due to the constraints of specific economic phenomenon. However, these pioneering efforts provide a comprehensive theoretical background and inspiration for successors. After Cho and Moon (1998), virtually no models of national competitiveness have been proposed. Conversely, these PCA models and their concepts have recently been applied successfully to various fields including the following: tourism competitiveness (Dwyer et al., 2000, 2002; Enright & Newton, 2004, 2005); seafood manufacturer competitiveness (Bess, 2006); data mining technology to identify competitiveness (Zanakis & Becerra-Fernandez, 2005); relationships between technological innovation and competitiveness (Guan et al., 2006; Solleiro & Castañón, 2005).

2.3.3 Summary

Reviewing the evolution of international trade theories can elucidate the relationships between RCA and PCA. The relationships are summarized as follows.

(i) The RCA indicates the industrial development trend and adjustment in a country based on its natural endowments (production factors). Thus, competitiveness based on RCA, at the international level, can be viewed as a long-turn (static) guideline in industrial development policy making. In contrast, Porter argued that production factors no longer play a critical role in the global economy of today. The PCA analysis explores the factors determining whether a specific industry can achieve success in a global competitive environment. Therefore, PCA competitiveness at the global level can be viewed as a short-term (dynamic) tactic for planning industrial strategy.

Additionally, RCA is also inadequate for explaining trade patterns such as the predominance of trade between developed and industrialized countries with similar endowments. Hence, employing policies to influence or improve RCA would only lead to inefficient industrial development. Porter suggested that RCA concepts should be replaced by a new paradigm, analysis of global industrial competitiveness.

(ii) The PCA analysis tends to focus on "dynamic competition," particularly technological change and innovation activity. The Porterian analysis assumes static efficiency during a given time period would be changed by rapidly developing technologies. Hence, competition is not perfect but rather a dynamic combined effect of new products, new marketing mechanisms, new production patterns and new market segments. The above considerations are quite different from those of exogenous comparative advantages theories but similar to those of endogenous comparative advantages theories.

(iii) The PCA analysis relies on historical data and experiential induction instead of formal economic language to construct the diamond model. The PCA model is easily understood and applied. Meanwhile, compared to RCA, PCA provides a comprehensive analytical framework of competetiveness by not only adopting the legitimacies of exogenous comparative advantages theories but also by accepting the outcomes of endogenous comparative advantages theories. According to Cho and Moon (2000), "Adam Smith is the pioneer of trade theory and Michael Porter is the pioneer of competitiveness theory."

2.4 Competitiveness and Evaluation Methodology

2.4.1 Definitions of Competitiveness

2.4.1.1 Composition of Competition

Competitiveness accompanies competition; without competition, competitiveness is nonexistent. Hence, defining competition requires an understanding of the reason for competition. George J. Stigler, the author of the "competition" entry in *The New Palgrave: A Dictionary of Economics*, edited by Eatwell et al. (1991), defined competition as "a rivalry between individuals, and it arises whenever two or more parties strive for something that all cannot obtain." The definition of competition requires understanding several other dimensions in addition to competitiveness: (1) competitors, i.e., competing with whom. Generally, when two or more independent and interested individuals (groups or nations) have interdependent interests, they may decide to collaborate or cooperate rather than compete with each other; (2) competing objects, i.e., something (e.g., profits, market share, material sources, idea innovation, service networks, customers satisfaction, etc.) that not all groups can obtain easily; without competing objects, no competition is possible; (3) competitive capability, i.e., independent interested individuals demonstrate their special characteristics and abilities during the competitive process; the more capable they are , the more easily they obtain competing objects; (4) competed results, i.e., competing objects are eventually allocated among competitors. If the results are not mutually satisfactory, competition may continue.

Based on these four dimensions of competition, it is important to note that each competitor seeks to enhance its competitive capability by specialization in its special characteristics or by differentiation of its products or services to successfully obtain the desired objective. If the competed results are not satisfied, it would once again prepare to participate in the four competition dimensions. Therefore, during any competitive cycle, each competitor shapes its competitiveness. The following discussion examines the relevant literature regarding competitiveness.

2.4.1.2 Definitions of Competitiveness

Unsurprisingly, there is no clear, standard definition of competitiveness or structural approach to understanding competitiveness. According to the ABI/Inform database, from 1985 to 2006, more than 4,000 regular papers regarding the concept of competitiveness were published in refereed journals. Of course, research in different disciplines with different perspectives of the concept and its implications for public and private sector decision making is a continuous undertaking. Thus, the lack of definition for competitiveness provides a broader research topic: developing a universally applicable definition of the concept. The above definition of competition offers a micro and a macro perspective of competitiveness. From a macro perspective (in Porterian terminology including industry-level and government-level), competitiveness enhances the prosperity of a nation by improving the real income of its citizens, whose performances comprise the social, cultural, and economic variables in international markets. Conversely, of course, from a micro perspective, the term mainly indicates a firm-level quality, i.e., firm-specific behaviors determine competitiveness. Any firm must provide products and services to its customers or clients to obtain returns (profits or market shares, and so on). Therefore, competitiveness at the firm level is mainly measured by the competitive capability of a firm to earn the competed results and to ensure its future development.

Because the focus of this dissertation is competitiveness in the tourist industry, competitiveness is viewed from a macro perspective. Table 2.1 lists several different macro perspectives of competitiveness proposed in the literature. His Majesty Treasury (1983) pioneered a formal definition of competitiveness in its annual economic progress report. Clearly, HM Treasury is concerned with economic performance, particularly market share and market size of a product, to evaluate national competitiveness. Scott and Lodge (1985) and Fajnzylber (1988) provided a similar analysis for HM Treasury. In 1985, the U.S. Government proposed a famous definition of competitiveness (Report of the President's Commission on Industrial Competitiveness, 1985) which assumed that the function of government is to maintain competitiveness, such as by ensuring a fair market, harmonizing supply and demand and increasing real income of citizens. Henceforth, Fagerberg (1988), The Economist (1994), Krugman (1994) and Durand et al. (1998) closely followed the U.S. Government proposition in defining competitiveness. In the 1990s, Newall (1992) was the first to consider both economic concepts and functions of government in a more complete definition of competitiveness. Newall proposed that competitiveness should include the issue of sustainable development. The Newall proposition deeply influenced the research of later scholars, institutions and organizations. For example, the European Commission (1994) and OECD (2000) both indicated that the competitiveness of a country should be measured by sustainable consideration.

Table 2.1 lists definitions based on the view that competitiveness is measured by market share and growth, improved quality of life for citizens and national sustainable development. Based on these definitions, shaping

Table 2.1 Literature review of definitions on competitiveness

Literature sources	Propositions
1. Economic perspective	
(i) His Majesty's Treasury (1983, p. 1)	"International competitiveness means the ability of a country's producers to compete successfully in world markets and with imports in its own domestic market. Competitiveness is generally measured by … the shares which a country attain in its markets, due allowance being made for its size and stage of development. Competitiveness in this very general sense comes to being synonymous with overall economic performance."
(ii) Scott and Lodge (1985, p. 3)	"…refers to a country's ability to create, produce, distribute and/or service products in international trade while earning rising returns on its resources."
(iii) Fajnzylber (1988, p. 12)	"Competitiveness is a country's capacity to sustain and expand its share of international markets and at the same time to improve its people's standard of living."
2. Government functions added	
(i) Report of the President's Commission on Industrial Competitiveness (1985)	"Competitiveness is the degree to which a nation can, under free and fair market conditions, produce goods and services that meet the test of international markets while simultaneously maintaining or expanding the real incomes of its citizens"
(ii) Fagerberg (1988, p. 355)	"..ability of country to realize central economic policy goals, especially growth in income and employment, without running into balance of payments difficulties."
(iii) The Economist (1994, p. 17)	"A competitive economy is one that exports goods and services at world prices."

(Continued)

Table 2.1 (Continued)

Literature sources	Propositions
(iv) Krugman (1994, p. 31)	"Competitiveness is our ability to produce goods and services that meet the test of international competition while our citizens enjoy a standard of living that is both rising and sustainable."
(v) Durand et al. (1998, p. 4)	"The notion of competitiveness is … the broadest approach consists of comparing macroeconomic performance and overall living standards, by generally focusing on productivity trends."
3. Combined economic perspective, government functions, and sustainable development	
(i) Newall (1992, p. 94)	"Competitiveness is about producing more and better quality goods and services that are marketed successfully to consumers at home and abroad. It leads to well paying jobs and to the generation of resources required to provide an adequate infrastructure of public services and support for the disadvantaged. In other words, competitiveness speaks directly to the issue of whether a nation's economy can provide a high and rising standard of living for our children and grandchildren."
(ii) European Commission (1994, p. 17)	"…the capacity of businesses, industries, regions, nations or supernational associations exposed, and remaining exposed, to international competition to secure a relatively high return on the factors of production and relatively high employment levels on a sustainable basis."
(iii) OECD (2000, p. 9)	"The competitiveness of a country is essential for the welfare of its citizens. It means output growth and high rates of employment in a sustainable environment."

competitiveness activities should include two principal items: resources and transformation. Resources include *inherited* (e.g. natural resources) and *created* (e.g. infrastructure) resources. Transformations imply the transformation of resources to obtain economic profits during the competitiveness-shaping processes. Of course, these definitions could be applied at different levels. At the firm level, competitiveness means creating new products, the value of which provides feedback to its shareholders. At the industry/national level, competitiveness provides new jobs and better living standards and increases the real income of its citizens, which eventually ensures sustainable development.

Competitiveness in the tourism industry, the focus of this dissertation, could be defined as "the competitive position (with high profits and constant growth) of the tourism industry of a nation relative to the global market of tourist industries in other nations, whether developed or developing countries, which therefore increases the real income and standard of living of its citizens."

2.4.2 Evaluation Methodology

According to previous competitiveness perspectives, competitiveness in a specific industry results from convergence of management practices, organizational modes in its country and the sources of competitive advantage in the industry. Thereby, competitiveness in an industry of a country is influenced by a range of qualitative and quantitative factors. The three most common measures of competitiveness in the literature (Guan et al., 2006) are cost-benefit analysis, resource-based viewpoints and ranking style (Porterian style). These measures are briefly reviewed below.

2.4.2.1 Cost-Benefit Analysis

Artto (1987) applied economic theories to demonstrate that competitiveness measurement could be determined by financial status and relative total costs, including (1) cost-competitiveness: the most common measurement based on unit labor costs; (2) price-competitiveness: used for heterogeneous markets and measured by relative selling price; (3) non-price competitiveness: measured by cost, price (or both) of a non-separable part. Artto employed all three dimensions of competitiveness in developing the concept of "total competitiveness" to measure competitiveness of an industry, which is based on total revenues minus total costs or simply net income. Further for a more accurate measurement, he developed the concept of relative total costs (total costs divided by net sales;

i.e., operational mastery) as a substitute for unit total costs (total costs divided by units sold). Henceforth, the cost-benefit analysis approach became mainstream in competitiveness evaluation research.

Oral (1986) constructed an industrial competitiveness model which analyzed three basic factors, namely, industrial mastery, cost superiority and political-economic environment. Oral (1993) and his colleagues (Oral & Reisman, 1988) both successfully implemented the proposed industrial competitiveness model to perform empirical research regarding the glass industry. His findings provide useful insight into competitive strategy formulation. Li (2000) applied the least square technique to construct simple regression models revealing the relationships between performance and competitive sources for Chinese manufacturers. However, the essential findings of Li are beyond the scope of cost-benefit analysis.

These cost-benefit analyses focused mainly on financial indicators, particularly at the firm level. Although they may have weaknesses in their technical assumptions of regression models of error terms, they do provide lists of competitive factors (without explaining the formation mechanism of competitiveness).

2.4.2.2 Resource-Based Viewpoints

Recently, resource-based analyses (Barney, 1991; Peteraf, 1993; Prahalad & Hamel, 1990; Wernerfelt, 1984) have been applied to explain the composition of competitiveness. Examined dimensions include organization management, manufacturing, marketing and environment. Wernerfelt (1984) suggested that most products require the services of several resources, and most resources can be used in several products. Hence, specifying a resource profile for a firm should reveal its optimal strategic activities. Prahalad and Hamel (1990) further argued that core competencies, particularly those which involve collective learning and are knowledge-based, are enhanced as they are applied. Such sources may provide both the basis and the direction of growth of the firm itself. The Prahalad and Hamel proposition enhanced the resource-based model developed by Barney (1991), by including two assumptions in the analysis and analyzing sources of competitive advantage. Barney employed four attribute criteria, namely, value, rarity, imperfect imitability and substitutability, as empirical indicators of the heterogeneity and immobility of firm resources and how to sustain competitive advantages. Peteraf (1993) applied the concept of "*rent*[2]" to gain insight into theoretical conditions (namely cornerstones) of proposed

---

[2] Earnings in excess of breakeven are called rents, rather than profits, if their existence does not induce new competition (Peteraf, 1993, p. 180).

resource-based models underlying competitive advantages. Peteraf also conducted well applications of his proposed model for both single business strategy and corporate strategy.

Those resource-based frameworks mainly focused on resources controlled by a firm, including assets, capabilities, organizational processes, firm attributes, information and knowledge to indicate the superiority of the very resource possessed by the firm. Similar to cost-benefit analyses, however, these frameworks are still limited to the firm level.

2.4.2.3 Ranking Style (Porterian Points)

However, recognizing which factor primarily affects competitiveness is still controversial. Particularly, measuring only a single performance criterion such as profitability or finance is insufficient to determine the excellence of an industry. Consequently, multifactor modeling was developed to measure competitiveness (Chakravarthy, 1986; Chin et al., 2003), which ranks market competitive position and identifies appropriate strategic combinations needed to sustain a stronger and reasonable competitive edge. In addition, as the globalization process continues, competitiveness is often presented by ranking style for comparison between countries. World Economic Forum (WEF, 2005) and International Institute of Management Development (IMD, 2005) have started to rate countries annually based on various competitiveness indicatorsThe IMD and WEF have produced the most extensive and widely publicized comparisons of national competitiveness via annual publications of WCY (World Competitiveness Yearbook) and GCR (Global Competitiveness Report), respectively. The GCR is an index for 117 countries containing data obtained from secondary sources and primary survey of various macroeconomic and microeconomic dimensions of national economies. The competitiveness score for each country is a synthesis of data for eight major factors, including openness, government, finance, infrastructure, technology, management, labor and institution (listed in Table 2.2). The WCY, which analyzes approximately 60 countries, is derived from data underlying socio-economic and political indicators and surveys of various international and individual country statistics. The competitiveness score for each country synthesizes all data into four major factors: economic performance, government efficiency, business efficiency and infrastructure (listed in Table 2.3). Importantly, both the GCR of the WEF and the WCY of the IMD are clearly based on PCA.

As Tables 2.2 and 2.3 demonsrate, these two reports analyze almost the same factors of competitiveness. However, they are quite different in the weight assigned to each factor. The WCY of the IMD uses a one-third/

Table 2.2 Factors of competitiveness (GCR, before 2001)

Factors	Descriptions
Openness	This factor measures openness to foreign trade and investment, openness to foreign direct investment and financial flows, exchange rate policy and ease of exporting.
Government	This factor measures the role of the state in the economy. This includes the overall burden of government expenditures, fiscal deficits, rates of public saving, marginal tax and overall competence of the civil service.
Finance	Finance measures how efficiently the financial intermediaries channel savings into productive investment, the level of competition in financial markets, the perceived stability and solvency of key financial institutions, levels of national saving and investment, and credit ratings given by outside observers.
Labor	This factor measures the efficiency and competitiveness of the domestic labor market. It combines a measure of the level of a country's labor costs relative to international norms, together with measures of labor market efficiency (e.g. obstacles to hiring and firing of workers), the level of basic education and skills, and the extent of distortive labor taxes.
Infrastructure	This factor measures the quality of roads, railways, ports, telecommunications, cost of air transportation and overall infrastructure investment.
Technology	This factor measures computer usage, the spread of new technologies, the ability of the economy to absorb new technologies and the level and quality of research and development.
Management	Management measures overall management quality, marketing, staff training and motivation practices, efficiency of compensation schemes and the quality of internal financial control systems.
(Civil) Institutions	This factor measures the extent of business competition, the quality of legal institutions and practices, the extent of corruption and vulnerability to organized crime.

Source: WEF (2000).

two-third balance between hard data (statistical indicators published publicly) and soft data (via survey activities). Clearly, the weighted assignment of factors is quite arbitrary and sometimes lacks theoretical support. Ranking style comparisons can be misleading if they are not based on a rigorous theoretical methodology (lack of explanations for factors selection) and measurement model (lack of suitable weights for each factor). Therefore, these two competitiveness reports often produce significant discrepancies in their rankings (Cho & Moon, 2000).

Table 2.3 Factors of competitiveness (WCY)

Factors	Descriptions
Economic performance	This factor measures the extent of its past economic performance, domestic economy, international trade, international investment, employment and prices.
Government efficiency	This factor measures the extent of government policies are conducive to competitiveness: public finance, fiscal policy, institutional framework, business legislation and societal framework.
Business efficiency	This factor measures the extent of enterprises are performing in an innovative, profitable and responsible manner: productivity and efficiency, labor market, finance, management practices and attitudes and values.
Infrastructure	This factor measures the extent of basic, technological, scientific and human resources meet the needs of business: basic infrastructure, technological infrastructure, scientific infrastructure, health and environment and education.

Source: IMD (2005).

Table 2.4 Growth competitiveness index (GCR, after 2001)

Indices	Descriptions
Growth competitive index	
(1) Technology index components	This index measures the extent of innovation, technology transfer, and information and communication technology.
(2) Public institutions index components	This index measures the extent of contract and law, corruption.
(3) Macroeconomic environment index components	This index measures the extent of macroeconomic stability, institution investor country credit rating, and government waste variable.

Source: WEF (2005).

To correct the above deficiencies, the WEF has introduced new indices since 2001, namely, *Growth competitive index* (GCI) (listed in Table 2.4). The GCI measures the ability of national economies to achieve long-term economic growth. Conversely, the WEF also provides a micro level index, the *Business Competitiveness index* (BCI), OR which measures a range of company-specific factors affecting efficiency and productivity at the micro level. The BCI measures two specific areas that are critical to the business

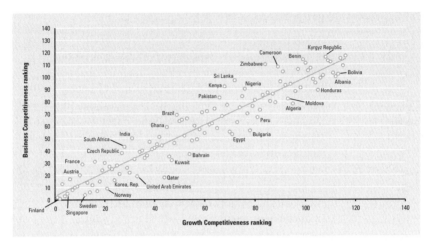

Fig. 2.2 Growth and Business Competitiveness rankings

Source: WEF (2005).

environment in each country: sophistication of company operations and strategies and quality of national business environment. The WEF has emphasized that the GCI and the BCI measure complementary dimensions of competitiveness; Fig. 2.2 reveals the high correlation between the two measures.

2.4.2.4 Summary

The evolving concept of competitiveness from RCA to PCA has produced varying measures of competitiveness (including cost-benefit analysis, resource-based points, and ranking reports from WEF to IMD), but consensus is lacking as to the best systematic analytical measure of competitiveness. Therefore, comparing these measures of competitiveness does not clearly indicate the inefficiencies that should be rectified and improved.

A continuing challenge for researchers examining the tourism research is whether the measures used accurately capture the "truth" (Ritchie, 1975). This dissertation therefore proposes suitable competitiveness indicators which enable a consistent comparison between countries and between industries in the tourism sector. These indicators should enable countries to quantify the competitiveness of their tourism industries and identify areas requiring improvement.

2.5 Tourism Competitiveness Researches

2.5.1 Overview of Tourism Competitiveness Researches

In many industrialized countries, the service sector, particularly international trade services, is an increasingly important "engine" of economic growth. Thereby, countries, cities and regions now take their role as tourist destinations very seriously and devote considerable effort and funds to enhancing their tourist image and attractiveness. Meanwhile, tourism researchers have begun to devote more attention to tourism destination competitiveness.

Poon (1993), the pioneer scholar in tourism competitiveness issues, indicated four key principles that any destination should follow if it is to be competitive: (1) put the environment first; (2) make tourism a leading sector; (3) strengthen the distribution channels in the marketplace; and (4) build a dynamic private sector. However, these principles are too broad to inspire any constructive suggestion to tourism stakeholders and policy makers. Deeper perspectives of destination competitiveness are needed.

The most widely accepted definition of tourism destination competitiveness is inherited from economic theory and focuses on market mechanisms and each component (including products and services) of tourism industry that could successfully maintain the attractiveness of a destination. Dwyer et al. (2000, p. 9; 2002, p. 328), in the most detailed study of tourism price competitiveness thus far, proposed that "competitiveness is a general concept that encompasses price differentials coupled with exchange rate movements, productivity levels of various components of the tourist industry and qualitative factors affecting the attractiveness or otherwise of a destination." Hassan (2000, p. 239) similarly indicated that "competitiveness is defined here as the destination's ability to create and integrate value-added products that sustain its resources while maintaining market position relative to competitors."

The other successors employed the concepts of PCA in a reappraisal of the tourism competitiveness issue. In 1993, Crouch and Ritchie performed an exploratory study for constructing an analytical framework to explain the dynamic evolution of competitiveness in international tourism. Chon and Mayer (1995) later amended the framework of Crouch and Ritchie by incorporating tourism-specific issues such as the intangible nature of tourism products/services and the substitute relationships between tourism products/services, as well as the renewability of tourism resources and externalities. Their proposed tourism competitiveness model employed five dimensions: appeal, management, organization, information and efficiency. However, the Chon and Mayer model was questioned regarding its substitute relationships between tourism products and services. To address this deficiency, Faulkner et al. (1999) performed an empirical qualitative study to identify the competitiveness of the South Australian domestic tourism market to reveal substitute relationships of tourism products (wine industry) and services (Murray River theme).[3]

Tourism competitiveness researches have also extensively examined destination image or attractiveness to identify the relative important benefits of attractive attributes. Gearing et al. (1974) developed a procedure for investors to select locations for hotels and related tourism facilities. Twenty-six tourism experts were asked to weight 17 quantitative measures of tourism attractiveness. Then, 65 tourist areas were ranked by scores based on those criteria. However, their research required that the criteria be appropriately established and that the evaluation procedure be properly explained. Hu and Ritchie (1993) employed a contextual approach analyzing vacation experiences to measure destination attractiveness. They found that people generally have more positive impressions about destinations they had visited. For destination image, Gallarza et al. (2002) developed a conceptual model by conducting a detailed review and taxonomy of tourism destination image measurements. Hsu et al. (2004) further implemented an empirical study to identify the tourism image of the State of Kansas to identify tourist destinations with limited comparative advantages. They concluded that not all image attributes influence the overall tourist impression of a destination, and significant overlap occurs among the four different attributes. Bonn et al. (2005) employed two categories of environmental attributes, destination atmospherics and destination service, to compare the destination image perceptions in three groups of visitors to Florida (in-state, non-Florida, and international). In contrast with Hu and Ritchie (1993), they found that international visitors have higher service and environmental standards when judging this destination compared to in-state and domestic visitors. Generally, while tourism services had been viewed as important elements of destination image, explicit attention should be paid to firms providing the services and to the factors affecting

---

[3] It is useful to refer the special issue of the journal *Tourism Management* (volume 21, number 1, February 2000) to view other regarding tourism competitiveness issue, for example, d'Hauteserre (2000) provided a successful tourism destination case of Foxwoods Casino Resort about managing competitiveness. He indicated that the visionary entrepreneurial activity and strategic management decisions are the basic power of its owners to analyze the destination's increasing competition for the entertainment and leisure dollar in the eastern U.S., then, modify its market strategies to acquire expected position. Exactly as d'Hauteserre said "its success is not some circumstantial fluke."

the competitiveness of these firms, i.e., whether it is a firm management issue or one of destination competitiveness (Buhails, 2000). However, Murphy et al. (2000) also indicated that both environmental conditions and infrastructure have a strong bearing on tourist perceptions, which in turn influence their assessment of destination competitiveness.

Recent tourism competitiveness research has employed two approaches. One is combining theories and concepts of PCA to re-consider tourism competitiveness issues. Representative is Enright and Newton (2004, p. 778; 2005, p. 340), who concluded that "a destination is competitive if it can attract and satisfy potential tourists, and this competitiveness is determined both by tourism-specific factors and a much wider range of factors that influence the tourism service providers." (2) The second incorporates a more precise measure to deal with the destination competitiveness issue rather than functional/physical attributes of destination attractiveness evaluation. Russo and van der Borg (2002, p. 632) enhanced and popularized the concepts of cultural tourism. They argued that "the cultural experience becomes a holistic process, where producer and consumer cohere in a gazer who identifies a symbolic significant." Therefore, for any destination, employing cultural infrastructure is useful, especially those with symbolic meaning, to maintain its attractiveness over time, even with scarce heritage assets. Several scholars have supported the idea that cultural tourism experiences of places are best understood by their symbolic signification. The representative cases are the "Legacy tourism" proposed by McCain and Ray (2003), and the "cross-cultural tourism: Hakka and non-Hakka tourists" proposed by Hou et al. (2005).

Here, it would be useful to summarize tourism competitiveness as the ability of a destination to create, integrate and deliver tourism experiences, including value-added goods and services considered to be important by tourists, which sustain resources while maintaining market position relative to other destinations.

2.5.2 Crouch and Ritchie's Contributions

In the late 1990s, Crouch and Ritchie (1999) published the most important work (till now) in the analysis of tourism competitiveness with their conceptual model of destination competitiveness (as Fig. 2.3). They claimed that the most competitive destination, on a sustainable basis, produces the best lifestyles and societal prosperity. Conversely, they applied the PCA framework to competitiveness research in tourism destinations, extensively spreading their focus from companies and products (services) to national service industries and national economies. Therefore, they believed that

Fig. 2.3 Conceptual model of destination competitiveness

Source: Crouch and Ritchie (1999).

destination competitiveness should be measured not only by capability to enhance lifestyles and societal prosperity but also by efficiency in resource allocation, which produces long-term economic prosperity. Their proposed model is structured in two layers. The external layer represents comparative advantages (resource endowments) and competitive advantages. The internal layer represents several major elements: (1) competitive environment; (2) global (macro) environment; (3) core resources and attractors (including physiography, culture and history, market ties, mix of activities, special events, and tourism superstructure); (4) supporting factors and resources (e.g., infrastructure, accessibility, facilitating resources, and enterprise); (5) destination management (such as marketing, service, information, organization, and resource stewardship); (6) qualifying determinants (e.g., cost, safety, location, and dependencies).

Their model provides a feasible and accurate model for competitiveness analysis of tourism destinations. However, there remain several dimensions to improve or enhance in specific situations. For example, the relative order of importance of major factors and categories of variables could not be accurately modeled. Secondly, the model does not analyze the effects of and interaction between comparative advantages, competitive advantages and tourism competitiveness. Finally, those major factors are examined in qualitative terms rather than quantitative terms. Restated, those qualitative relationships could be established rigorously by quantitative analysis. Meanwhile, many countries still lack complete databases.

This dissertation provides a framework for systematic analysis of tourism competitiveness, including exogenous comparative advantages (RCA1), endogenous comparative advantages (RCA2) and PCA. Additionally this study provides detailed illustrations of its specific operational interactions effects among RCA, PCA, tourism management operational regulations, the domestic environment restrictions and global environment requirements (see Fig. 1.2). These models are given in the following sections, beginning with indicators of tourism competitiveness.

References

Arrow KJ (1962) The economic implications of learning by doing. The Review of Economic Studies 29:155–173.

Artto EW (1987) Relative total costs—An approach to competitiveness measurement of industries. Management International Review 27:47–58.

Barney JB (1991) Firm resources and sustainable competitive advantages. Journal of Management 17:99–120.

Baron J, Kemp S (2004) Support for trade restrictions, attitudes, and understanding of comparative advantage. Journal of Economic Psychology 25:565–580.

Bess R (2006) New Zealand seafood firm competitiveness in export markets: The role of the quota management system and aquaculture legislation. Marine Policy 30:367–378.

Bonn MA, Joseph SM, Dai M (2005) International versus domestic visitors: An examination of destination image perceptions. Journal of Travel Research 43:294–301.

Buhails D (2000) Marketing the competitive destination of the future. Tourism Management 21:97–116.

Chakravarthy BS (1986) Measuring strategic performance. Strategic Management Journal 7:437–458.

Chin KS, Pun KF, Lau H (2003) Development of a knowledge-based self-assessment system for measuring organizational performance. Expert Systems with Application 24:443–455.

Cho DS (1994) A dynamic approach to international competitiveness: The case of Korea. Journal of Far Eastern Business 1:17–36.

Cho DS, Moon HC (1998) A nation's international competitiveness in different stages of economic development. Advances in Competitiveness Research 6: 5–19.

Cho DS, Moon HC (2000) From Adam Smith to Michael Porter: Evolution of competitiveness theory. World Scientific Publishing Co: Singapore.

Chon KS, Mayer KJ (1995) Destination competitiveness models in tourism and their application in Las Vegas. Journal of Tourism Systems and Quality Management 1:227–246.

Cohen SS (1994) Speaking freely. Foreign Affairs 73:194–197.

Crouch GI, Ritchie JRB (1999) Tourism, competitiveness, and societal prosperity. Journal of Business Research 44:137–152.

d'Hauteserre AM (2000) Lessons in managed destination competitiveness: The case of Foxwoods Casino Resort. Tourism Management 21:23–32.

Davis DR, Weinstein DE (2003) Market access, economic geography and comparative advantage: An empirical test. Journal of International Economics 59:1–23.

Dixit AK, Stiglitz JE (1977) Monopolistic competition and optimum product diversity. The American Economic Review 67:297–308.

Dunning JH (1993) Internationalizing Porter's diamond. Management International Review 33:7–15.

Durand M, Madaschi C, Terribile F (1998) Trends in OECD countries' international competitiveness: The influence of emerging market economies. Economics Department Working Papers No. 195, OECD: Paris.

Dwyer L, Forsyth P, Rao P (2000) The price competitiveness of travel and tourism: A comparison of 19 destinations. Tourism Management 21:9–22.

Dwyer L, Forsyth P, Rao P (2002) Destination price competitiveness: Exchange rate changes versus domestic inflation. Journal of Travel Research 40: 328–336.

Eatwell J, Milgate M, Newman P (1991) The new palgrave: A dictionary of economics (four volumes series). The Macmillan Press Ltd: UK.

Enright MJ, Newton J (2004) Tourism destination competitiveness: A quantitative approach. Tourism Management 25:777–788.

Enright MJ, Newton J (2005) Determinants of tourism destination competitiveness in Asia Pacific: Comprehensiveness and universality. Journal of Travel Research 43:339–350.

The Economist (1994)   The economics of meaning. The Economist, April 30, 331(7861):17–18.

European Commission (1994) Competitiveness Advisory Group, Enhancing European Competitiveness, 2nd Report to The President of The Commission, OOPEC: Luxembourg.

Fagerberg J (1988) International competitiveness. The Economic Journal 98: 355–374.

Fajnzylber F (1988) International competitiveness: Agreed goal, hard task. CEPAL Review 36:7–23.

Faulkner B, Oppermann M, Fredline E (1999) Destination competitiveness: An exploratory examination of South Australia's core attractions. Journal of Vacation Marketing 5:125–139.

Fisher EON, Kakkar V (2004) On the evolution of comparative advantage in matching models. Journal of International Economics 64:169–193.

Freeman C (1994) The economics of technical change. Cambridge Journal of Economics 18:463–514.

Gallarza MG, Saura IG, García HC (2002) Destination image: Towards a conceptual framework. Annals of Tourism Research 29:56–72.

Gearing CE, Swart WW, Var T (1974) Establishing a measure of touristic attractiveness. Journal of Travel Research 12:1–8.

Grant RM (1991) Porter's competitive advantage of nations: An assessment. Strategic Management Journal 12:535–548.

Greenaway D (1993) The competitive advantage of nations by Michael E. Porter. Kyklos 46:145–146.

Guan JC, Yam RCM, Mok CK et al. (2006) A study of the relationship between competitiveness and technological innovation capability based on DEA models. European Journal of Operational Research 170:971–986.

Hassan SS (2000) Determinants of market competitiveness in an environmentally sustainable tourism industry. Journal of Travel Research 38:239–245.

Heckscher E (1919) The effect of foreign trade on the distribution of income. Economisk Tidskrift 21:497–512.

Hirsch WZ (1956) Firm progress radios. Econometrica 24:136–143.

His Majesty's Treasury (1983) International competitiveness. Economic Progress Report 158:1–5.

Hou JS, Lin CH, Morais DB (2005) Antecedents of attachment to a cultural tourism destination: The case of Hakka and non-Hakka Taiwanese visitors to Pei-pu, Taiwan. Journal of Travel Research 44:221–233.

Hsu CHC, Wolfe K, Kang SK (2004) Image assessment for a destination with limited comparative advantages. Tourism Management 25:121–126.

Hu YZ, Ritchie JRB (1993) Measuring destination attractiveness: A contextual approach. Journal of Travel Research 32:25–34.

International Institute for Management Development (IMD) (2005) The World competitiveness yearbook 2005. Lausanne: Switzerland.

Ivanova IM, Arcelus FJ, Srinivasan G (1998) Assessment of the competitiveness position of the Latin American countries. International Journal of Commerce & Management 8:7–32.

Kim D, Marion BW (1997) Domestic market structure and performance in global markets: Theory and empirical evidence from U.S. food manufacturing industries. Review of Industrial Organization 12:335–354.

Krugman P (1994) Competitiveness: A dangerous obsession. Foreign Affairs 73:28–46.

Krugman P (1979) Increasing returns, monopolistic competition and international trade. Journal of International Economics 9:469–479.

Lancaster KJ (1980) Intra-industry trade under perfect monopolistic competition. Journal of International Economics 10:151–175.

Leontief W (1953) Domestic production and foreign trade: The American capital position re-examined. Proceedings of the American Philosophical Society 97:332–349.

Li LX (2000) An analysis of sources of competitiveness and performance of Chinese manufacturers. International Journal of Operations & Production Management 20:299–315.

Linder SB (1961) An essay on trade and transformation. John Wiley: New York.

List F (1983/1837) The natural system of political economy (Translation and edition by W. O. Henderson). Cass: London.

Lucas RE (1988) On the mechanism of economic development. Journal of Monetary Economics 22:3–42.

McCain G, Ray NM (2003) Legacy tourism: The search for personal meaning in heritage travel. Tourism Management 24:713–717.

Meliån-Gonzålez A, Garcia-Falcón JM (2003) Competitive potential of tourism in destinations. Annals of Tourism Research 30:720–740.

Moon HC, Rugman AM, Verbeke A (1998) A generalized double diamond approach to the international competitiveness of Korea and Singapore. International Business Review 7:135–150.

Murphy P, Pritchard MP, Smith B (2000) The destination product and its impact on traveler perceptions. Tourism Management 21:43–52.

Newall JE (1992) The challenge of competitiveness. The Business Quarterly 56:94–100.

OECD (2000) The competitiveness of European industry: 1999 Report. Working Document of The Services of The European Commission. COM(1999) 465, OECD: Paris.

Ohlin B (1933) Interregional and international trade. Harvard University Press: Cambridge.

Oral M (1986) An industrial competitiveness model. IIE Transactions 18:148–157.

Oral M (1993) A methodology for competitiveness analysis and strategy formulation in glass industry. European Journal of Operational Research 68:9–22.

Oral M, Reisman A (1988) Measuring industrial competitiveness. Industrial Marketing Management 17:263–272.

Pavitt KLR (1980) Technical innovation and british economic performance. Macmillan: London.

Peteraf MA (1993) The cornerstones of competitive advantages: A resource-based view. Strategic Management Journal 14:179–191.

Poon A (1993) Tourism, technology and competitive strategy. CAB International: Wallingford (UK).

Porter ME (1980) Competitive strategy: Techniques for analyzing industries and competitors. The Free Press: New York.

Porter ME (1985) Competitive advantages: Creating and sustaining superior performance. The Free Press: New York.

Porter ME (1990) The competitive advantages of nations. The Free Press: New York.

Prahalad CK, Hamel G (1990) The core competence of the corporation. Harvard Business Review 68:79–91.

Report of the President's Commission on Industrial Competitiveness (1985) Global competition: The new reality. U.S. Government Printing Office: Washington DC.

Ricardo D (1971/1817) On the principles of political economy and taxation. Penguin: Baltimore.

Ritchie JRB (1975) Some critical aspects of measurement theory and practice in travel research. Journal of Travel Research 14:1–10.

Romer P (1990) Endogenous technological change. Journal of Political Economy 98:S71–S102.

Rugman AM, D'Cruz JR (1993) The double diamond model of international competitiveness: The Canadian experiences. Management International Review 33:17–39.

Russo AP, van der Borg J (2002) Planning considerations for cultural tourism: A case study of four European cities. Tourism Management 23:631–637.

Ryan R (1990) A grand disunity. National Review 42:46–47.

Schumpeter J (1912) The theory of economic development. Duncker & Humblot: Leipzig. Reprinted in 1934 by Cambridge: Harvard University Press, and added subtitle "An inquiry into profits, capital, interest and the business cycle."

Scott BR, Lodge GC (1985) U.S. competitiveness in the world economy. Harvard Business School Press: Boston M A.

Sim LL, Ong SE, Agarwal A (2003) Singapore's competitiveness as a global city: Development strategy, institutions and business environment. Cities 20: 115–127.

Skidelsky R (1992) John Maynard Keynes: The economist as saviour, 1920–1937 (Vol. 2). Macmillan London Limited: UK.

Smith A (1994/1776). An inquiry into the nature and causes of the wealth of nations (modern library). Random House: New York.

Solleiro JL, Castañón R (2005) Competitiveness and innovation systems: The challenges for Mexico's insertion in the global context. Technovation 25:1059–1070.

Thurow LC (1994) Microchips, not potato chips. Foreign Affairs 73:189–192.

Vernon R (1966) International investments and international trade in the product cycle. Quarterly Journal of Economics 81:190–207.

Wernerfelt B (1984) A resource-based view of the firm. Strategic Management Journal 5:171–180.

World Economic Forum (WEF) (2000) The global competitiveness report 2000. WEF: Switzerland.

World Economic Forum (WEF) (2005) The global competitiveness report 2005. WEF: Switzerland.

Xepapadeas A, de Zeeuw A (1999) Environmental policy and competitiveness: The Porter hypothesis and the composition of capital. Journal of Environmental Economics and Management 37:165–182.

Yang XK (1994) Endogenous vs. exogenous comparative advantage and economies of specialization vs. economies of scale. Journal of Economics 60:29–54.

Yang XK, Zhang DS (2000) Endogenous structure of the division of labor, endogenous trade policy regime, and a dual structure in economic development. Annals of Economics and Finance 1:211–230.

Zanakis SH, Becerra-Fernandez I (2005) Competitiveness of nations: A knowledge discovery examination. European Journal of Operational Research 166:185–211.

3 Research Methods

Chapter 2 presented a literature review regarding the evolution of competitiveness (including exogenous comparative advantage theories, endogenous comparative advantage theories, and competitive advantage frameworks) and competitiveness evaluation approaches The review provides a theoretical background needed to understand the issue of tourism competitiveness. Since a tourist is required to travel to a destination to receive the destination service, the fundamental product in tourism is the destination experience. Competition focuses primarily on the tourism destination and secondarily on its relevant industries such as airlines, hotels, facilitates and other tourism services. Competition may also be the so-called inter-industry competition, which is dependent upon and derived from the process of choosing between alternative tourist destinations. To analyze the tourism competitiveness of a country, a city, or a region, the following questions must be answered: "What factors influence the decision making of tourists?"; "What indicators are most useful for objective analysis by tourism planners?" and "Is there a feasible evaluation methodology or standard operation procedure to assist tourism planners in strategic planning?".

The rest of Chap. 3 verifies the research framework of tourism competitive information; secondly, a series of hypotheses are proposed regarding interactions between RCA and PCA for improving decision making; finally, an evaluation methodology and procedure is proposed.

3.1 Evaluative Indicators for Tourism Competitive Information

Evaluative indicators of tourism competitive information examine three internal dimensions and two external dimensions. The three internal dimensions are the following.

W.-C. Hong, *Competitiveness in the Tourism Sector.* Contributions to Economics,
doi: 10.1007/978-3-7908-2042-3_3, © Physica-Verlag Heidelberg 2008

3.1.1 Comparative Advantages

This section examines resource endowments of a tourism destination in any country. In addition, based on the literature review in Chap. 2, comparative advantages are classified as exogenous comparative advantages and endogenous comparative advantages. The principal classification criterion is the permanence of those resource endowments among global tourism countries. Thus, resource endowments which cannot be changed by any endogenous factor in the economic system of the corresponding country, are so-called "exogenous comparative advantages." Conversely, those resource endowments easily changed by endogenous factors (such as physical/human capital investment, technological innovation, and so on) from correspondent country economic system are so-called "endogenous comparative advantages."

Definition 1: *Tourism exogenous comparative advantages are those resource endowments which cannot be changed by any endogenous factor in the correspondent country economic system. Conversely, tourism endogenous comparative advantages are those resource endowments which are more easily changed by endogenous factors, such as physical/human capital investment and technological innovation, in the correspondent country economic system.*

(1) Exogenous Comparative Advantages

As mentioned above, **natural resources** (including *climate, scenery, landscape* and *minerals*) of a destination are seldom changed or improved by scientific advancements. Such endowments include mild climate (e.g., Yunnan, China; Nantou, Taiwan), romantic scenery (e.g., Hangzhou, China; A-Li Mt., Taiwan), a Karst topography landscape (e.g., Guilin, China) and weathered landscapes (e.g., The Grand Canyon National Park, U.S.). Of course, such endowments are attractive to tourists and are undoubtedly comparative advantages when tourists choose a holiday resort.

Cultural/heritage resources (including *history, music, paintings, folklore, temple sites* and *special events*) create the principal memorable experiences of a destination for tourists. Hence, unique or heterogeneous tourism experiences (such as learning, understanding of other cultures, cultural change, and stronger cultural identity) produced by cultural resources are also the source of tourism attractiveness. For example, destinations designated as "World Cultural and Natural Heritage" sites by

UNESCO[1] are the classic representative examples, such as Old Town of Lijiang (Yunnan, China), Memphis and its Necropolis or the Pyramids from Giza to Dahshur (Egypt). Another representative example is the local festivals or celebrations in a specific destination. Generally, celebration is combined with folklore such as The Songkran Festival (Thailand), All Saints Day (New York, U.S.) and Gion Matsuri (Kyoto, Japan). Additionally, these celebrations may be combined with a specific religious event such as an Islamist pilgrimage mission (Mecca, Saudi Arabia) or going aboard to worship the birthday of Matzu (Taichung, Taiwan).

For **capital resources** (including *annual fixed investment* and *fixed growth rate in investment per year*) consideration, if a destination has abundant capital resources, it is easily not only to seek for cooperation with respect to capital-intensive tourism infrastructures and related software, but also to provide essential assistance to tourism development to achieve economies of scale. For example, Las Vegas (Nevada, U.S.) has relatively abundant capital resources. Not only did federal government investment in the Hoover Dam help produce hotel-casino dollars after the dam was built, but additional FDI was also attracted by the casino-tourism industry.[2] Abundant capital resources became the development engine of Las Vegas and enabled the city to provide more services and related facilities than other gaming destinations. In the same manner, abundant capital resources shape the comparative advantages of correspondent countries.

(2) Endogenous Comparative Advantages

As mentioned previously, tourism endogenous comparative advantages contain such resources that can be improved or changed to suit the

---

[1] United Nations Educational, Scientific and Cultural Organization (UNESCO) was founded on November 16, 1945. It is working to create the conditions for genuine dialogue based upon respect for shared values and the dignity of each civilization and culture. This role is critical, particularly in the face of terrorism, which constitutes an attack against humanity. The world urgently requires global visions of sustainable development based upon observance of human rights, mutual respect and the alleviation of poverty, all of which lie at the heart of UNESCO's mission and activities. Its web-site is as following, http://portal.unesco.org/en/ev.php-URL_ID=29008&URL_DO=DO_TOPIC&URL_SECTION=201.html.

During the 17th session of The General Conference, UNESCO had authorized the famous "Convention Concerning the Protection of the World Cultural and Natural Heritage" to institutionally provide protection of this heritage at the national level often remains incomplete.

[2] More details could be referred the Las Vegas Official web-site, http://www.lasvegasnevada.gov/ FactsStatistics/history.htm.

requirements of a destination for developing competitiveness. **Human resources** (including *education in commerce, training on job*, and *protection of natural resources*) of a destination are the primary representative examples. As noted by Arrow (1962), it is important to encourage human capital investment in tourism related operation management, particularly steadily evolving from labor (i.e., efficiently learning by doing or on the job training) while acquiring and accumulating knowledge successfully. For example, via *commercial education courses*, tourism resources/facilities, destination managers and employees are integrated into a united organization. Acquiring expertise in total service (including flowchart, tourists' demand, tourists' satisfaction, and so on) by providing tourist services should be the core of commercial education courses. Additionally, in accordance with Yang (1994), specialization of employees, *training on job*, especially for their regular operations, would enhance professional efficiency. For instance, while listening attentively to the "Past Anecdotes" of France Royals from the short-fat tourist guide of Chateau de Versailles and Louvre, the most striking impression is, in addition to the detailed commentary, the personal responsiblility for his job and the pride in his country displayed by the tour guide. This factor is the key to maintaining the competitiveness of a great nation and becomes unshakeable as time goes by. Finally, *protection of natural resources* ensures the preservation of specific natural resources and reveals their deserved comparative advantages from a long-term perspective. Examples are scarce resources like the Great Wall (China) or the Mona Lisa (the famous painting of Leonardo da Vinci).

Note 1: *It is useful to enhance endogenous tourism comparative advantages via learning-by-doing activities and specialization processes in tourism related operation management, particularly steadily evolving from labor (education in commerce, training in operation management, and protection of natural resources) while acquiring, accumulating knowledge successfully.*

According to the spillover effect proposed by Lucas (1988), any successful destination attractiveness mode can be delivered to another via exporting these successful knowledge accumulations or by introducing key knowledge applications, so-called **knowledge resources**. Of course, while introducing this successful knowledge accumulation to a new destination (spillover effect occurs), the knowledge resources must be revised to meet the demand of this specific destination. The revision approaches contain, firstly, *expanding existed exogenous resources.* For example, Disney Company has exported its successful attractiveness mode to Hong Kong and has established branch site in Hong Kong. The popular Disneyland experience expands the original exogenous resources of Hong Kong. The second step is *localizing existing exogenous resources.* For example, Disneyland, like the Aboriginal Culture Land in Taiwan, has been introduced to many foreign countries. The success of these amusement parks depends on localizing existing exogenous resources to meet the demands of Taiwan or to reveal local characteristics.

Note 2: *Another useful approach to enhancing endogenous tourism comparative advantages is the spillover effect. Any successful destination attractiveness mode can be delivered to another via exporting these successful knowledge accumulations or introducing key knowledge application. The spillover effect causes exported knowledge accumulation and experiences to expand the original exogenous resources of the target destination. However, introducing key knowledge applications must be localized to existing exogenous resources to meet the demands of the target destination or to reflect local characteristics.*

Finally, the Schumpeter (1912) concept of innovation processes is appropriate for analyzing endogenous comparative advantage caused by **technological innovation**. Based on the Schumpeter model of innovation processes, technological innovation in the tourism service context requires the following elements: operation mode innovation (new services), special events creation (new market) and electronic information resources (new method of services). *Operation mode innovation* of a destination is always based on its available resources, from its internal total quality management activities, external benchmarking learning and even integrating upstream/downstream businesses as strategic alliance. This process implies that total members of a destination should always optimize their service cycle (standard operation procedure) for tourists, and any feasible process for improving projects to provide tourists with more convenient service, and information collection from the same businesses to seek any cooperation opportunity to enhance its disadvantages. *Electronic information resources*, different from traditional information providing and transmitting, not only provide immediate information to potential tourists, but also transmit prompt information when tourists start their tourism schedule. These resources include well-designed and stimulating on-line guide to the destination, downloadable guide map, a transportation timetable querying system, convenient world-wide-web (WWW) network service providing. During the implementation of the above resources, disharmony and fierce competition between the new and old, a diversity of growth rates and profits rates among different sections of a destination, and continual reallocation of labor and capital investment activities are expected. On the other hand, a destination can also enhance its attractiveness via a *special events creation* process. As Romer (1990) indicated, innovation plays an essential role in translating new knowledge into commodities with practical value. Therefore, any destination would be inspired by folklore or legend which gives tourists a sense of adventure should organize events to attract potential tourists. An example is the harvest festival inspired the kindly assistance of the Corn Spirit in Britain, The ritual sacrifice of an animal traditionally represented the continuity of the Spirit. Eventually, the practice led to the Harvest Festival organized by churches beginning in 1843 (The Harvest Festival in the early Autumn in UK).[3] England employed this folklore to create a special event which then became a cultural resource. In fact, almost every special event or celebration epitomizes folklore or legend.

3.1.2 Competitive Advantages

As shown in the literature review in Chap. 2, the efforts of PCA pioneers provided a comprehensive theoretical background and inspiration for application. The PCA view is that national prosperity can be created or be improved by factor allocations. Therefore, this part mainly indicated that a tourist destination is able to use its resource endowments effectively for attracting potential tourists. Thus, competitive advantages provide a deeper insight into the reallocation of different tourism resource endowments. The destination then has a feasible approach (strategy) to modifying its comparative advantages.

---

[3] The celebration of Harvest in Britain dates back to pre-Christian times when the success of the crop governed the lives of the people. Saxon farmers offered the first cut sheaf of corn to one of their gods of fertility, in order to safeguard a good harvest the following year. The last sheaf was thought to contain the Spirit of the Corn, and its cutting was usually accompanied by the ritual sacrifice of an animal – often a hare caught hiding in the corn. Later, a model hare, made from straw, was used to represent the continuity of the Spirit. This practice eventually led to the making of plaited "corn collies", symbolizing the goddess of the grain. These were hung from the rafters in farmhouses until the next year. When the harvest was in, a celebratory supper was held to which the whole community was invited. The now widespread practice of celebrating Harvest Festival in churches began in 1843, when the reverend Robert Hawker invited parishioners to a special thanksgiving service at his church at Morwenstow in Cornwall. This led to the long-practised custom of decorating churches with home-grown produce.

Definition 2: *Tourism competitive advantages arise from effectively using the resource endowments of a tourism destination to attract potential tourists. Additionally, competitive advantages provide insight into the reallocation strategy of different tourism resource endowments to modify existing comparative advantages.*

Competitive advantages of a tourism destination in this study are assumed to have the following dimensions.

(1) **Infrastructure investments** (including *accessibility design, accommodations, transportation systems* and *characteristic food*) of a destination are the most important functional bases, also known as physical resources (in Porter's terminology is so-called *advanced factors*). Firstly, these infrastructures generally provide rational expectations for potential tourists planning their tourism schedule. For example, a convenient transit system for connecting with scheduled flight (arrival and departure) and local transportation is expected to offer a schedule convenient for tourism. Additionally, the destination tourist track of those characteristic resorts, foods and cultural heritages could be designed based on the average length of stay and required accommodation. Thus, the accessibility design of a destination is composed of many related services accurately supporting, and become the prior competitive advantages formation in infrastructure investments issues. Secondly, as mentioned above, prompt transportation systems support, including local transportation systems (metropolitan transit systems, taxi and boats for city tour, off-shore island or rural, and scenic railway) and global airport systems, play a critical role in the accessibility of a destination and thus become another competitive advantage of infrastructure investment. Meanwhile, effective accommodation support is critical in the accessibility of a destination. Examples are panoramic scenic views and an isolated and secluded atmosphere (Dubai Burj Al Arab is the most representative). Finally, characteristic foods, including special ingredients and cooking technologies, could be developed and innovated based on both the foods themselves and tourism market forces. Potential tourists are attracted to characteristic foods. For example, Ching & Han Royal Dynasty Feast is representative of traditional Chinese food.

Note 3: *Infrastructure investments of a destination are the most important functional advanced factors. Many infrastructures are from related supplier industries supporting and providing efficient, rapid access to tourism services. Therefore, during the servicing process, they are important for transmitting information (such as new ideas, new insights and suppliers' innovations) from firm to firm to innovation, upgrading innovation and internationalization.*

(2) **Strategic planning to market ties** (including *building tourism linkages with related characteristics* and *creative activities*) of a destination are the secondary functional institutional investments which can attract potential tourists (in Porter's terminology is so-called *internationalization of domestic demand*). Firstly, ethnic ties, implying the same language and the same race, are the basis for tourism demand due to the desire of tourists to visit relatives, such as those tourists who work or live abroad with regular home leave. Additionally, the concept of ethnic ties leads to creation of ethnic related activities such as the Ancestries Memorial Ceremony of the Chinese Nation in Xi'an (China) and in Taiwan. However, ethnic ties for some country without long period of time establishing have no chance of using. A viable strategy is constructing institutional market ties. This means internationalizing domestic demand. For example, by holding international academic conferences, workshops, congresses and symposiums or by sponsoring world exhibitions, fairs and expositions, countries can increase domestic demand (tourism services) by holding or sponsoring business, academic, and leisure activities to attract demanders. Establishing market ties can generally generate steady flow of visitors and some level of economic growth. Meanwhile, according to the Porter view that domestic rivalry often pressures firms to improve quality and service and innovate new products and processes to ensure long-term preservation of advantages, the tourism industry has an incentive to encourage strong domestic rivalries while business ties are being formed, such as by encouraging domestic rivalries to sponsor a world fair or an international conference.

Note 4: *Market ties of a destination are the secondary functional investments in terms of internationalization of domestic demand to institutionally attract potential tourists. Ethnic ties, the primary market ties of a destination, often lead to creation of ethnic-related activities for providing sympathetic responses in visiting tourists. Additionally, ethnic ties can induce domestic rivalries which promote domestic demand to potential demanders by constructing institutional business ties such as by hosting international academic conferences or world fairs.*

(3) **Maintaining resources** (including *regular maintenance schedule, protection institution, seasonal peak load adjustment* and *protection technological innovation*) of a destination are also important issues in acquiring competitive advantages. As Porter pointed out, although an abundant factor may destroy competitive advantage, selected disadvantages in factors often contribute to competitive success if implementing influential strategy and innovation activities. Therefore, a destination with limited tourism resources must implement a regular monthly, quarterly and yearly

maintenance schedule. Particularly for fragile cultural artifacts, buildings, landscapes and for general tourism resources subject to harsh weather conditions, it is necessary to organize special institutions or agencies to assume responsibility for protecting these tourism resources. Additionally, it is important to plan the monthly, quarterly or annual tourist restrictions to avoid overuse of tourism resources in the seasonal peak period and avoid them lying idle in the slack season. Hence, effective seasonal marketing promotion strategy could be employed to optimize tourist flow.

The above discussion refers to destination protection. However, innovation activities are also required to use technology to protect tourism resources, such as microfiche technology to preserve historical documents, advanced architectural engineering or landscaping to preserve fragile historical buildings and minimize damage from harsh weather conditions.

(4) **Monitoring resources allocations** (including *resources I/O analysis, exhausting monitor system*, and *emergency response system*) of a destination is an important issue in competitive advantages sustainability. This work, firstly focused on establishing a monitoring system to track the annual input/output performances of tourism resources. An additional task was identifying unreasonable allocation segments such as LISO (large input, small output). Then, based on the corresponding development target, arrange a suitable I/O ratio to reallocate tourism resources. Secondly, this work also establishes a monitoring system to track the circumstances of tourism resources intentionally or unintentionally exhausted by tourists. Examples include publishing tourism white papers analyzing a destination such as fixed investments for tourism resources, stock forecasts for tourism resources and sustainable development efforts and improvements. Finally, this work establishes an emergency response system to provide emergency and rescue services for tourist areas to respond to forest fires, accidents, etc.

(5) **Growth and development** (including *economic growth* and *public security system development*) constitute the socio-economic status of a destination which can robustly support tourism related facilitates (infrastructures) and tourism safety network system. Economic growth not only reveals the economic development efforts of a destination but also objectively presents its capability for tourist industry support and attractiveness to potential investors. Generally, a destination with rapid/ continued economic growth attracts FDI in key industries then generates market ties (including ethnic ties, business ties and leisure ties) to promote a steady tourist flow. On the other hand, the public security of a destination can provide a safer environment for tourists. Encountering thief

UNIVERSITY OF HERTFORDSHIRE LRC

or other crimes while traveling not only leaves tourists with a poor impression of the very destination but also decrease his/her subsequent evaluation. Thus, tourists would be reluctant to revisit the destination due to deteriorating public security. Examples are the 1998 riots in Jakarta (Indonesia) and the 1994 Murder Accident of Thousand Island Lake in Zhejiang (China). Both incidents substantially reduced tourism. Therefore, development of a reliable public security system improves competitive advantage.

(6) **Operational performance effectiveness** (including *one-stop tourism package services*) of a destination is the primary motivation of tourists. As indicated by Porter, sophisticated home buyers of a country lead firms to easily acquire competitive advantage. Therefore, a destination may become capable of providing operational performance effectiveness because of its sophisticated domestic tourists and their high expectations in comparison to other destinations. Therefore, sophisticated domestic tourists not only create an incentive to deliver excellent tourist services, they also provide an early warning of deteriorating tourist services or the need for change. The concept of "one-stop tourism package services" was developed to address this consideration. For example, by integrating total tourism services (pleasure parks, hotels, restaurants, resorts, tourism fruit farms, and so on) of a destination into a selection menu or list, tourists can determine suitable item services when making their journey arrangements. Disney Company is a representative example of one-stop tourism package services.

Note 5: *Operational performance effectiveness of a destination mainly depends on the sophistication of domestic tourists and their high level of demanding expectations in comparison to other destinations. According to the Porter analysis, sophisticated domestic tourists not only provide incentive to review tourism precise services delivering performances, but also serve as an early warning indicator of mainstream tendencies in worldwide tourism services or the need for transition or change. The concept of one-stop tourism package of a destination was developed to address this consideration.*

(7) **Facilitating resources created** (including *public services* and *financial institutions*) of a destination provides convenience to tourists. Public services include those providing tourists with information or detailed travel information while traveling in this destination. Examples are rapid post delivery services (including postcard, regular mail, and physical tourist souvenirs), prompt and high quality telecommunication (domestic calls and international phone calls), barrier-free public environment design.

Financial institutions provide tourists with related financial services during the retention period, such as travel checks, currency exchange and money remittance. Generally, high tourist satisfaction increases the attractiveness of a destination.

3.1.3 Tourism Management

According to the Porter view, the proper role of government is creating an environment that stimulates industries or companies to acquire competitive advantage such as providing high quality education and training, public goods, support services and reduced transaction costs. Further, Porter indicated that governments can also influence firm strategy, structure, and rivalry through such approach as market regulation, tax policy and antitrust laws. In the tourism context, the tourism management component focused on those management activities that enhance the comparative advantages and competitive advantages mentioned above. Thus, tourism management activities provide appropriate assistance to strengthen the quality and effectiveness of different tourism resource endowments. Scientific approaches (strategies) are then provided to manage the attractiveness of a destination to (potential) tourists.

Definition 3: *The tourism management component must focus on those management activities that provide appropriate assistance in strengthening the quality and effectiveness of different tourism resources or endowments (comparative advantages and competitive advantages). Additionally, destination scientific approaches (strategies) are needed to manage the attractiveness of a destination to (potential) tourists. Tourism management activities mainly include resource stewardship training, marketing, organization and regulations, businesses integration, information providing and services.*

(1) **Resource stewardship training**. As mentioned above, the cultural heritage of a destination may be represented by fragile, buildings or landscapes subject to harsh weather conditions. Therefore, special institutions or agencies must be organized to protect important tourism resources. Resources stewards for a destination, i.e., resources managers, should be trained to professionally implement effective maintenance procedures for those resources, including *subtle nurturing technologies* and *philosophical education in the concepts of long term sustainable competitiveness*. These training activities combined with scholars in the professional field of protection and preservation of historical/cultural relics is an adaptable approach to enhancing the responsibilities and professional abilities of

resources managers. For example, the training of workers to maintain the Terracotta Army (Bing Ma Yong) in Xi'an involved experts from many universities and research institutes in Xi'an.

(2) **Marketing** is the most traditional activity of a destination for promoting its tourism resources such as natural resources, cultural/heritage resources, other attractions. However, as mentioned in the previous discussion of comparative advantages and competitive advantages, marketing activities should primarily focus on: (a) *tourism products or services development* (e.g., special events creation, market ties establishments); (b) *reasonable pricing policies* for adjusting tourist amounts between seasonal peak period and slack season; (c) *distribution channel to target markets* (well market segment based on riche of a destination); (d) developing *one-stop tourism package services* by integrating total tourism services into a selection menu or list for tourists determination.

(3) **Organization and regulations** of a destination are responsible for destination development in a wide range of opportunities to ensure destination competitiveness. *The management organization* plays the key role not only in decision-making for creating destination attractiveness based on its comparative and competitive advantages but also in suitable strategies planning for FDI on tourism-related development. Practically, however, the management organization is often required to collaborate with governmental bureaus or even with interest groups to conduct collaboration development projects such as urban and regional development bureaus investment banking. Therefore, *well related regulations* ensure these collaboration projects operate smoothly, efficiently, and effectively. Meanwhile, those regulations also encourage management organizations to provide more suitable strategic planning of tourism development in shaping its competitive advantages with respect to future challenges. In fact, in the tourism competitiveness context, management organization and related regulations could be viewed as the role of "government" in the Porter diamond model.

(4) **Businesses or firm integration** implies sharing operational resources (e.g., rents of shop fronts, employees, and fixed costs of facilities) and intangible assets (e.g., attractiveness of potential tourists, goodwill, and efficiency in operations) to provide more comprehensive tourism services. In tourism industries, the production of commodities and services and the development of new products require the use of specialized equipment or support services such as landscape development and tourist souvenir designs. An individual firm is usually unable to provide a large

enough investment (tourist amounts) for these services to keep the suppliers in business. A localized business cluster can solve this problem by bringing together many firms to provide a large enough investment (tourist amounts) to support specialized suppliers. Additionally, a cluster of businesses can create a pooled market for workers with highly specialized skills (tourist guide) needed in the tourism industry. Thus, the advantage for a destination is the reduced likelihood of labor shortages. Further, workers with these specialized skills are less likely to become unemployed.

Therefore, tourism businesses integration could develop to form *specialized-supplier-linkages, labor market pooling* and even *knowledge spillover* (Arrow, 1962; Lucas, 1988), which would then reduce manufacturing costs (tourism commodities and services). As Krugman (1979) suggested, "with the effects of regional agglomeration, trade may be a way of extending the market and allowing exploitation of scale economies". A cluster of tourism businesses or firms located in a specific geographic area can acquire a competitive advantage through increased efficiency.

Finally, returning to the tourism management context, business integration is encouraged in a tourist destination to obtain agglomerative synergy and to avoid excessive competition in the same tourism commodities or services. Of course, business agglomeration should avoid establishment of monopolies.

Note 6: *Tourism businesses or firm integration implies sharing the operation resources and intangible assets to provide more comprehensive tourism services. The integration could develop to form specialized-supplier-linkages, labor market pooling, and knowledge spillover, then, reduce the costs of manufacturing to obtain agglomerative synergy, to avoid excessive competition on the same tourism commodities or services providing.*

(5) **Information providing** by a destination refers to information systems that provide destination managers with *tourist information* (including tourists situations, needs, and satisfaction); to monitor the *tourism resources information* (including the stocks of tourism resources, the status and warning of those fragile cultural heritages, buildings, and related landscapes); to track the *related products information* (including the related product development, performances of related industries, businesses or firms); and to make *particular decisions*. Information systems of a destination are also responsible for regularly announcing key market and performance information to its members, investors, tourists, competitors and other related organizations. Such information is essential to ensure the

productivity, effectiveness and efficiency of a destination. Particularly, newly emerging tourist destinations, the the learning by doing approach (reviewing, monitoring performances) proposed by Arrow (1962) is best for improving performance.

(6) **Services** of a destination include *hard resources* (infrastructure, natural, cultural resources) and *soft resources* (all services from attendant, waiter, steward, and porter; and all facilitating resources providing). Those services are emphasized to provide the most possible satisfaction to tourists via all compositions of tourism packages (experiences). Destination managers should pay close attention to such aspects by attempting firstly to ensure the accessibility of hard resources such as by seamlessly transporting tourists to their desired tourist tracks, providing convenient transportation systems, an adequate selection of accommodations and prompt tour guides or commentators. Secondly, managers must ensure delivery of complete information regarding soft resources, such as a barrier-free interface for accessing each component of total tourism packages (experiences). Finally, destination services include such aspects as providing the convenience of inter-modal transfers for each component of tourist packages sold.

The remaining two dimensions of external indicators examine environmental effects such as domestic and global environment conditions. As Porter indicated, chance events create discontinuities allowing shifts in competitive position. Chance events may lead to failure of previous competitors and provide opportunities for new firms to acquire competitive advantage under new conditions. Additionally, chance events often have little to do with circumstances in a nation and are often largely outside the power of firms (and often the national government) to influence. Therefore, in a tourism competition context, chance events often change destination environment conditions (including natural resources destroyed, operational modals adjustments, and uncertainty of management increased), thus increasing or decreasing competitive advantages of a destination. Environment conditions include both exogenous factors and endogenous factors. The former mainly indicates discontinuities in chance events; conversely, the latter mainly indicates circumstances that can be changed by effective decision making, strategic planning, or policy changes .Nevertheless, environment conditions can be classified into two parts: domestic environment conditions and global environment conditions.

Definition 4: *Tourism environment conditions are composed of exogenous factors and endogenous factors. Exogenous environment conditions mainly indicate the discontinuities of chance events that cause previous*

competitive destinations to fail and provide the opportunity for a new des-
tination to acquire a competitive advantage under new conditions. Con-
versely, the endogenous environment conditions mainly indicate the
circumstances that can be changed by decision making, strategic planning
or policy change.

3.1.4 Environment Conditions

(1) Domestic Environment Conditions

As mentioned above, **chance events** affecting circumstances of a destination are largely outside its power to influence. In the tourism competition
context, chance events are mainly composed of spread of disease, deple-
tion of natural resources and significant events in world financial markets.
The **spread of a disease** (SARS, bird flu, foot-and-mouth disease, etc.)
may cause tourist anxiety because of the possibility of transmission during
the journey and the speed of its spread. Extensive media coverage may add
to the anxiety. Any destination would have reduced attractiveness during
such a period. For example, during the Asian SARS outbreak period in
2003, the most severely affected countries were China, Hong Kong, Singapore and Vietnam (McKercher & Chon, 2004; Wilder-Smith, 2006). The
outbreak cost those four economies are over \$20 billion in lost GDP, and
tourist arrivals fell by 70% or more across the rest of Asia. Additionally,
the growth of the broader travel and tourism economy, as measured by
global tourism spending as well as capital investment, slowed from 5 to
2.9%[4] in the following years. **Natural resource deterioration** is another
uncertain domestic environment condition possible affecting attractiveness
of a destination. Deterioration of natural resources is usually caused by
natural disasters (e.g., September 21 Earthquake, South Asia Tsunami,
New Jersey Hurricane Katrina, etc.) and, less frequently, armed conflict
(e.g., Iraq war). For example, the 7.3 magnitude September 21 Earthquake
(Huang & Min, 2002) sapped the national economy. The GDP growth rate
in the fourth quarter of 1999 fell from 5.7 to 5.3% and surely dealt a sharp
blow to the Taiwan tourism industry. Additionally, the worst impact was
suffered by the international tourism sector, as evidenced by the sharp reduction in tourist visits during the disaster period, frightening away many
potential tourists. Thus, during the January–August period of 1999, visitor
arrivals were only 15% that of the same period in the previous year. Of

---

[4] More tourism lost analysis could be found in Wilder-Smith (2006) and McKercher
and Chon (2004).

course, cancellation of hotel rooms, airline seats, concert hall seats, coach seats, dining and banquets caused additional loss in tourism revenue. Finally, **significant events in world financial markets** refer to circumstances that reduce the value of a national currency. Thus, the deteriorating economy after the 1999 earthquake led to unemployment, rising prices and food shortages. Eventually, their combined effects severely impacted tourist arrivals and the tourism industry. Overseas tour operators may, in some crisis conditions, be required to evacuate passengers or cancel schedules. The Southeast Asian Financial Crisis (Henderson, 1999) is a well known example.[5] The tourism industries of the Asian region all suffered from the economic crisis in 1997. During that period, many tour operators were committed to prices fixed at pre-devaluation exchange rates and were reluctant to reduce prices to reflect currency devaluations of 20–40%. Global arrival figures for 1997 reflected the difficult market conditions in the growth rate decline from 5.6 to 2.8%. Eventually, East Asia and Oceania were the worst hit region, with a reduction in visitors and spending of 1.2% and 3.8% respectively. Asian intra-regional tourism is estimated to have fallen by 10%.

Conversely, domestic environment conditions may also involve circumstances that can be changed by decision making, strategic planning or policy changes, namely **superstructure changes**. In the tourism competition context, domestic environment conditions consist mainly of political climate changes, ethnic tension harmonization, laws or regulatory support and cultural diversification. **Political climate changes** are the stable political climates needed to encourage economic development (Clements & Georgiou, 1998), such as the opening of the Chinese economy in 1978. Attracting international tourists to earn foreign exchange becomes a basic national policy. Of course, this political climate is conducive to tourism development by enhancing competitiveness. **Ethnic tension harmonization** requires harmoninzing unnecessary ethnic tensions because international tourists are composed of all races in the world. Ethnic tensions such as hostility directed at Chinese communities in Southeast Asian can only reduce the attractiveness of a destination. **Laws or regulations supporting** means that laws of a destination robustly support development of tourism competitiveness such as Environment Pollution Prevention Act, Fragile Cultural and Natural Heritage Protection Act. Generally, laws or regulatory support always reveal the political tendencies of a destination with

---

[5] More Southeast Asian Financial Crisis analysis on tourism could be referred the special issue of the journal Current Issues in Tourism (volume 2, number 4) in 1999.

respect to attitudes to tourism development. Finally, **cultural diversification** is often all-embracing for all potential tourists. Thus, it can also increase the attractiveness or shape the unique characteristics of a destination. Domestic environment conditions are needed to showcase a destination as a place to live, trade with, invest in or do business with, i.e., provide international understanding of the destination.

Note 7: *Domestic environment conditions are chance events that affect the circumstances of a destination largely outside its power of influence. Examples are spread of disease, deterioration of natural resources and significant world financial events. Also included are circumstances that can be changed by decision making, strategic planning, or policy change, namely* **superstructure changes***, consisting mainly of political climate changes, reduction of ethnic tension, laws or regulations supporting and cultural diversification.*

(2) Global Environment Conditions

For global environmental conditions, **accidental events** or **expected events** create discontinuities that cause previous competitors to fail and provide opportunities for a new destination to acquire competitive advantage under new conditions. The so-called **accidental events** imply unexpected events such as **Terrorist Attack** (e.g., September 11 Event in 2001,[6] Bali Event in 2002, etc.) and **Global Epidemic Disease** (e.g., SARS in 2003, bird flu, foot-and-mouth disease since 2001 in UK, etc.). In contrast, **Economic Sanctions** and **Wars** are events that can be expected in advance. For example, the September 11 even severely affected the U.S. tourism industry. Air travel as well as hotel occupancy declined more than 50% (Goodrich, 2002). Therefore, in the tourism competition context, global environment conditions must be considered to provide more peaceful atmospheres such as democracy communique, humanism promotion and global collaboration in anti-terrorism activities. Any new tourism destination can employ these measures to enhance the attractiveness of its tourism products and services to potential tourists.

---

[6] On Tuesday morning, September 11, 2001, 19 suicide hijackers took control of four United States commercial airplanes and crashed them, respectively, into the Twin Towers of the World Trade Center (WTC) in New York City, the Pentagon in Washington, DC, and in a field in Somerset County, west of Pittsburgh, Pennsylvania. An estimated 5000–6000 people were killed. The cost of the tragedy, in terms of rebuilding, is estimated at about $105 billion (CNN Television News Report, October 5, 2001).

Note 8: *Global environment conditions* *mainly imply* *chance events,* *which create discontinuities that lead any new destination could employ them to acquire competitive advantage under new conditions, such as* *Terrorism Attack,* *Global Epidemic Disease,* *Economic Sanctions,* *and* *Wars.*

3.2 Influential Effects of Tourism Competitive Information

Section 3.1 introduced each component of the proposed competitiveness evaluation model for the tourism industry. Further, it is important to describe the dynamic interaction effects to enrich the content of the proposed model. The dynamic interaction effects of the proposed model are composed of two causal origins of interaction, namely RCA-originated influential effects and PCA-originated influential effects. These two influential effects are discussed below.

3.2.1 RCA-Originated Influential Effects

RCA-originated influential effects (Fig. 3.1) mainly indicate that exogenous comparative advantages and endogenous comparative advantages provide robust support for strategic enhancement of PCA. Meanwhile, tourism management, the third of the internal indicators determining tourism competitiveness of a destination, plays the role of catalyst to assist implementation of RCA-originated influential effects. Its detailed effects, including exogenous comparative advantages and endogenous comparative advantages, can be analyzed as follows.

1. Exogenous comparative advantages. Natural/cultural endowments firstly provide useful support for promoting infrastructure investment to exploit the tourist attraction of a target destination (real line in Fig. 3.1). An example is a special transportation system for a specific climate, scenery, or landscape, such as a cable railway system for high mountains and virgin forests. Additionally, characteristic foods and accommodations could also be inherited from cultural resources of a destination such as famous historical stories, folklore, special events or traditional celebrations. The Ching & Han Royal Dynasty Feast is the most representative example.

Influential Effect 1: *Natural or cultural endowments provide useful support for promoting infrastructure investment to develop the unique characteristics of a target destination as a tourist attraction.*

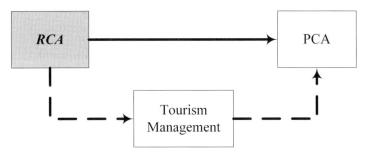

Fig. 3.1 RCA-originated influential effects

Secondly, well cultural endowments also provide useful support to plan suitable strategies for establishing market ties. For example, by employing abundant cultural/heritage resources to hold traditional cultural activities, exhibitions, fairs, or expositions to attract ethnic ties and market ties re-lated demanders. Finally, well endowments could provide resources for maintaining and well allocation considerations which directly enhance the sustainability of the PCA of a destination.

Influential Effect 2:   *Well endowments provide useful support for planning suitable strategies for establishing market ties.*

In the process of RCA-originated influential effects, tourism management contributes direct, prompt, and suitable assistance (dotted line in Fig. 3.1), such as marketing, strategic planning and stewardship training for transpor-tation systems design, characteristic food and accommodation services, transmission of cultural/heritage resources to acceptable types of cultural activity and arrangement of resource maintenance and allocation.

Influential Effect 3:   *Effective tourism management (e.g., marketing strat-egy planning, stewardship training, resource trans-mittal and maintenance) simultaneously provide useful, direct, prompt and suitable helps to Com-petitive advantages (RCA-originated influential effects).*

2. Endogenous comparative advantages. On the other hand, well improvable tourism resources would firstly provide useful support in assisting strategic planning to form market ties (real line in Fig. 3.1). For example, by promoting special events and expanding (localizing) exogenous resources to encourage the regular observance and cele-bration of festivals and ceremonies to introduce ethnic ties or market ties to potential tourists.

Influential Effects 4: *Well improvable tourism resources (special events creation, expanding exogenous resources) would provide useful support to strategies planning for developing market ties.*

Secondly, effective development of human resources would also provide effective and efficient resources maintenance and well allocation considerations which would directly enhance the sustainability of a destination PCA. Examples are improved technology for protecting and nurturing natural resources as well as education and training courses for new workers in natural resource protections. Finally, technological innovation (operational mode innovation and electronic information resources) would also increase the satisfaction with operational performance effectiveness and probably accelerate the implementation of public and financial services.

Influential Effects 5: *Effective development of human resources (e.g., education and training courses) and technological innovation (e.g., operational mode innovation and electronic information resources) provide effective resource maintenance, protection and nurturing, which directly enhance the sustainability of a destination PCA.*

Similarly, in this influential effects process, tourism management can play the role of catalyst to provide suitable assistance (dotted line in Fig. 3.1) such as: (1) marketing strategy planning for special events creation and expanding (localizing) exogenous resources to establish a tradition of new festivals and ceremonies; (2) stewardship training by scholars in the professional field to protect natural resources and develop education programs in preservation technology; (3) novel information systems providing complete soft resources information, and convenience of inter-modal transfers for each component of tourisms.

Influential Effects 6: *Effective tourism management] (e.g., special events creation strategies, professional stewardship training for natural resource protections and nurturing, novel information systems) play the role of catalyst to enhance competitive advantages (RCA-originated influential effects).*

3.2.2 PCA-Originated Influential Effects

The PCA-originated influential effects (Fig. 3.2) mainly indicate that PCA would provide strategic supports for value-added creation to enhance RCA. Similarly, tourism management would also play the role of catalyst in assisting implementation of PCA-originated influential effects. The following analysis examines the detailed effects of enhancing RCA, including exogenous comparative advantages and endogenous comparative advantages, respectively.

1. Enhancing exogenous comparative advantages. Effective infrastructure investment in target destination characteristics would inversely enhance the attractiveness of natural, cultural and heritage resources of a destination (real line in Fig. 3.2). For example, highly accessibility transportation systems and convenient accommodation services of a destination would not only increase tourist satisfaction, but also produce profound personal experiences or impressions which would enhance the popularity of a site and increase public appreciation. From a long term perspective, it could also lead to establishment of another famous characteristic tourism resource. A representative example is the development of Hong Kong as a famous tourism/shopping destination.

Influential Effects 7: *Infrastructure investment (e.g., high accessibility transportation systems, convenient accommodations services) would provide impressions to enhance the attractiveness of natural, cultural, and heritage resources.*

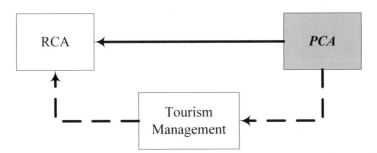

Fig. 3.2 PCA-originated influential effects

Secondly, the attractiveness of specific cultural resources of a destination can be enhanced by promoting foods and activities themselves such as by linking the provenances of those foods and activities with famous historical stories, folklore or special events. From a long-term perspective, identifying characteristic foods and activities can also lead to establishment of famous festivals or ceremonies which would attract tourists. The Songkran Festival in Thailand, (Japan) Gion Matsuri in Kyoto, and going abroad to worship the birthday of Matzu in Taichung (Taiwan) are representative examples. Finally, economic growth and enhanced public security would also increase fixed touris-related investment which would directly enhance the sustainability of a destination RCA.

Influential Effects 8: *Strategic planning to develop market ties (e.g., linking the provenance of characteristic foods and promoting activities associated with famous historical stories, folklore, or special events) enhances the attractiveness of a specific cultural resource.*

In the process of PCA-originated influential effects, tourism management contributes direct, prompt and suitable assistance (dotted line in Fig. 3.2) such as promotion strategy planning and stewardship training to emphasize profound tourism experiences or impressions of highly accessible transportation systems, convenient accommodations, characteristic foods and activities of a destination to enhance its popularity and public praise. Via marketing activities, stewardship training to increase the concept of responsibility and honor for working job can help developing characteristic tourism resources.

Influential Effects 9-1: *Well specified tourism management abilities on emphasizing tourism experiences (e.g., highly accessible transportation systems, convenient accommodations services, characteristic foods, and activities creation) to enhance its historical popularity and public praise.*

Influential Effects 9-2: *Well specified tourism management abilities to instill the concepts of responsibility and honor for working job would form another famous characteristic tourism resource.*

2. Enhancing endogenous comparative advantages. Conversely, via providing infrastructure services, planning market ties strategies and designing one-stop tourism package services would deeply find out real tastes of (potential) tourists (real line in Fig. 3.2). Such findings

would be inversely related to issues of human resource improvement, provide more insights into expanded or localized natural resources and inspire new directions for special events creation. Of course, tourism management would also help to implement the actions mentioned above (dotted line in Fig. 3.2).

Influential Effects 10-1: *Infrastructure, market tie strategies and facilitating package services would identify areas requiring improvement in human resources.*

Influential Effects 10-2: *Infrastructure, market ties strategies, and facilitating package services would provide more spread insights to expand or localize possessed natural resources.*

Influential Effects 10-3: *Infrastructure, market ties strategies and facilitating package services would inspire new directions for special events creation.*

3.3 Evaluation Methodology and Procedure

As mentioned in Sect. 2.4.2, many measures of competitiveness (e.g., cost-benefit analysis, resource-based points, and ranking reports from WEF to IMD) have been proposed. However, consensus is lacking as to the best systematic analytical structure for theoretically analyzing competitiveness. Therefore, considering the limitations or shortcomings of complex qualitative factors for competitiveness measurements, a ranking method for competitiveness measurements such as the annual reports of WEF and IMD had recently gained popularity. Meanwhile, for tourism considerations, tourism global competitiveness is most accurately measured not only by quantitative indicators but also by qualitative factors. Thus, a method producing a questionable ranking of tourism competitiveness would not be useful. Particularly in terms of qualitative factors, differences in ranking method would not elucidate what inefficiencies should be rectified and improved.

This section mainly suggests a corresponding evaluation methodology and procedure for tourism global competitiveness model (see Fig. 3.3). First, it is necessary to reexamine the problem of verifying these indicators, how they interact, and how to evaluate weights of the indicators.

3.3.1 Evaluation Indicators

The literature reviews in Sects. 2.1, 2.2 and 2.3 indicate the extensive influence of economic and management perspectives on construction of competitiveness models. In the meanwhile, the diverse views yield a more comprehensive framework for analyzing tourism global competitiveness. As discussed in Sects. 3.1 and 3.2, the verified indicators in the proposed model are primarily classified into three dimensions based on the competitiveness evolution perspectives described in previous sections, namely, *comparative advantage* (Sects. 2.1 and 2.2), *competitive advantage* (Sect. 2.3) and *tourism management* (Sect. 2.3). Secondly, other dimensions of verified indicators measure environmental considerations, namely, *domestic environment conditions* and *global environment conditions* (Sect. 2.3), to provide a more generalized perspective and consistent comparison between tourist destinations (and between industries). Furthermore, it is important to describe the dynamic interactive effects between these indicators. As introduced in Sect. 3.2, the interactive effects in the proposed model are causal origins of interaction, namely RCA-originated and PCA-originated.

The process of verifying these indicators and interactive effects among indicators would be based not only on models of RCA theories and empirical adjustments but also on the propositions of PCA theories, debates and adjusted models (shown in Fig. 3.3). Sixty-six indicators are verified to evaluate the overall tourism competitiveness performance of a destination, 20 for comparative advantages performance evaluation, 18 for competitive advantages performance evaluation, 17 for tourism management performance evaluation and 11 for environment conditions performance evaluation. Details of total verified indicators are listed in Table 3.1.

3.3.2 AHP to Evaluate Weights of Indicators

As mentioned above, the 66 indicators would contain numerous qualitative factors. Several effective alternative methodologies have been developed to measure qualitative factors. For example, most representative approaches in the field of tourism destination image (TDI) are known as (1) open ended questions procedure (Dann, 1996; Echtner & Ritchie, 1993); (2) focus group approach (Driscoll, Lawson & Niven, 1994; Fakeye & Crompton, 1991); (3) in-depth interviews/discussions with experts (Selby & Morgan, 1996; Bramwell & Rawding, 1996). In contrast with quantitative analysis, it requires a longer period of qualtitative data analysis when conducting any one of these three approaches. However, in the tourism context, accurately evaluating the weights of tourism global competitiveness model is important. Because the sources of a destination/country is much limited and is often requested to focus on the appropriate improvement or needed enhancement rectifications works for the most important indicator. Thus, determining the weight of each indicator is the most important issue in the following analysis.

To determine the weighting of both qualitative and quantitative indicators, the analytic hierarchy process (AHP) developed by Saaty (1977, 1980 and 1990) is employed to determine the relative importance of these 66 indicators (also see the second half of Fig. 3.3). The AHP is a powerful and flexible decision making process for setting priorities and making the best decision. By integrating different measures into a single overall score for ranking alternative decisions, analyzing survey data by pair-wise comparison judgments then synthesizing the results, AHP not only helps decision makers arrive at the best decision, but also provides a clear rationale for why the decision is best.

Applying the AHP approach requires constructing a hierarchical decision schema by decomposing the decision problem into its evaluation dimensions and detailing indicators. The importance or preferences of the evaluation dimensions (or detailing indicators) are then examined by pair-wise comparison in the hierarchy. Additionally, the parameters are estimated by pair-wise comparisons between the importance of the evaluation dimension or detailing indicator in the function using data provided by each responder. Making comparisons is a question of which of the two dimensions is more important as well as how much more important. The following shows the steps of analysis in the decision-making process using the AHP method:

Step 1: Define the decision problem and goal.

Step 2: Structure the hierarchy from the top through the intermediate to the lowest level which usually contains a list of alternatives.

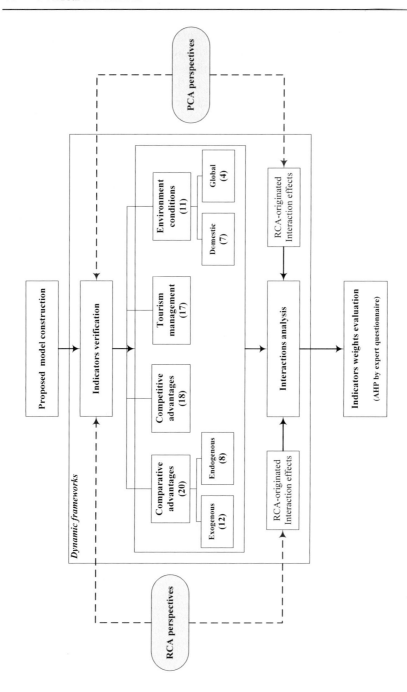

Fig. 3.3 Evaluation indicators verification procedure

Table 3.1 Total indicators of tourism global competitiveness evaluation model

Goal	Evaluation dimensions		Detailing indicators	Authors
Tourism competitiveness evaluation model	(Exogenous) Comparative advantages	Natural resources	(1) Climate (2) Scenery (3) Landscape (4) Minerals	Crouch and Ritchie (1999) Gearing et al. (1974) Hassan (2000) Ritchie (1975) Crouch and Ritchie (2000)
		Cultural/heritage resources	(5) History (6) Music (7) Paintings (8) Folklore (9) Temple sites (10) Special events	Gearing et al. (1974) Hassan (2000) Hou et al. (2005) Hu and Ritchie (1993) McCain and Ray (2003) Stevens (1992)
		Capital resources	(11) Annual fixed investment (12) Fixed growth rate in investment per year	Chon and Mayer (1995) Crouch and Ritchie (1999) Hassan (2000)
	(Endogenous) Comparative advantages	Human resources	(13) Education in commerce (14) Training on job (15) Protection of natural resources	Arrow (1962) Crouch and Ritchie (1999) Yang (1994)
		Knowledge resources	(16) Expanding existed exogenous resources (17) Localizing existed exogenous resources	Crouch and Ritchie (1999) Lucas (1988)
		Technological innovation	(18) Operation mode innovation (19) Electronic information resources (20) Special events creation	Crouch and Ritchie (1999) Romer (1990) Schumpeter (1912)
	Competitive advantages	Infrastructure investments	(21) Accessibility designing (22) Accommodations (23) Transportation systems (24) Characteristic food	Crouch and Ritchie (1999) Gallarza et al. (2002) Gearing et al. (1974) Hassan (2000) Hu and Ritchie (1993) McCain and Ray (2003) Russo and van der Borg (2002)
		Strategic planning to market ties	(25) Building tourism linkages with related characteristics (26) Creative activities	Crouch and Ritchie (1999) Poon (1993) Porter (1985, 1990)

(Continued)

Table 3.1 (Continued)

Goal	Evaluation dimensions		Detailing indicators	Authors
Tourism competitiveness evaluation model	Competitive advantages	Maintaining resources	(27) Regular maintain schedule (28) Protection institution (29) Seasonal peak load adjustment (30) Protection technological innovation	Crouch and Ritchie (1999) Dwyer et al. (2000, 2002) Porter (1985, 1990)
		Monitoring resources allocations	(31) Resources I/O analysis (32) Exhausting monitor system (33) Emergence response system	Crouch and Ritchie (1999) Dwyer et al. (2000, 2002) Porter (1985, 1990)
		Growth and development	(34) Economic growth (35) Public security system development	Crouch and Ritchie (1999) Enright and Newton (2004, 2005) Porter (1985, 1990)
		Operational performance effectiveness	(36) One-stop tourism package services	Crouch and Ritchie (1999) Porter (1985, 1990)
		Facilitating resources created	(37) Public services (38) Financial institutions	Crouch and Ritchie (1999) Porter (1985, 1990)
	Tourism Management	Resources stewardship training	(39) Subtle nurturing technologies (40) Philosophical education in the concepts of long term sustainable competitiveness	Arrow (1962) Buhails (2000) Crouch and Ritchie (1999) Lucas (1988) Porter (1985, 1990) Yang (1994)
		Marketing	(41) Tourism products or services development (42) Reasonable pricing policies (43) Distribution channel to target markets (44) One-stop tourism package services developing	Bramwell and Rawding (1996) Buhails (2000) Crouch and Ritchie (1999) Dann (1996) Porter (1985, 1990)

Goal	Evaluation dimensions		Detailing indicators	Authors
	Tourism Management	Organization and regulations	(45) Management organization (46) Well related regulations	Buhails (2000) Crouch and Ritchie (1999) Porter (1985, 1990)
		Businesses or firms integration	(47) Specialized-supplier-linkages (48) Labor market pooling (49) Knowledge spillover	Arrow (1962) Buhails (2000) Crouch and Ritchie (1999) Krugman (1979) Lucas (1988) Porter (1985, 1990)
		Information providing	(50) Tourists information (51) Tourism resources information (52) Related products information (53) Particular decisions	Arrow (1962) Buhails (2000) Crouch and Ritchie (1999) Porter (1985, 1990)
		Services	(54) Hard resources (55) Soft resources	Crouch and Ritchie (1999) Porter (1985, 1990)
	(Domestic) Environment conditions	Chance events	(56) Spread of disease (57) Natural resources deteriorated (58) Significant world financial exchange markets events	Crouch and Ritchie (1999) Henderson (1999) Huang and Min (2002) McKercher and Chon (2004) Murphy et al. (2000) Porter (1985, 1990) Wilder-Smith (2006)
		Superstructure changes	(59) Political climate changes (60) Ethic tensions harmonization (61) Laws or regulations supporting (62) Cultural diversification	Clements and Georgiou (1998) Crouch and Ritchie (1999) Murphy et al. (2000) Porter (1985, 1990)
	(Global) Environment conditions	Accidental events	(63) Terrorism Attack (64) Global Epidemic Disease	Crouch and Ritchie (1999) Goodrich (2002) Murphy et al. (2000) Porter (1985, 1990)
		Expected events	(65) Economic Sanctions (66) Wars	

Step 3: Matrices of pair-wise comparisons are constructed (size $n \times n$) for each of the lower levels with one matrix for each element in the level immediately above by using a relative scale measurement. The decision maker has the option of expressing his or her intensity of preference on a nine-point scale. If two criteria

are of equal importance, a value of 1 is given in the comparison while a 9 indicates an "Absolute importance" of one criterion over the other. Additionally, intermediate values (e.g., 2, 4, 6 and 8) imply intermediate values between adjacent judgments for example, "8" implies the compromising important position between "Demonstrated importance" and "Absolute importance". The following table (Table 3.2) shows the measurement scale defined by Saaty (1977, 1980 and 1990). Its use is based upon research by psychologist George Miller (1956), who indicated that decision makers were unable to consistently repeat their expressed gradations of preference finer than "seven plus or minus two."

Step 4: Computing eigenvalue by the relative weights of criteria and the sum to all weighted eigenvector entries corresponding to those in the next lower level of the hierarchy.

Step 5: Consistency and consequence weights analysis.

Pair-wise comparison data can be analyzed using the eigenvalue technique. Using these pair wise comparisons, the parameters can be estimated. The right eigenvector of the largest eigenvalue of matrix **A** (see Eq. (3.1)) constitutes the estimation of relative importance of attributes.

$$\mathbf{A} = \begin{bmatrix} 1 & w_1/w_2 & \cdots & w_1/w_n \\ w_2/w_1 & 1 & \cdots & w_2/w_n \\ \vdots & \vdots & \ddots & \vdots \\ w_n/w_1 & w_n/w_2 & \cdots & 1 \end{bmatrix} \qquad (3.1)$$

If matrix **A** is consistent (i.e., $a_{ij}=a_{ik}a_{kj}$ for all $i,j,k=1,2,...,n$), then **A** contains no errors (the weights are already known) and

$$a_{ij} = w_i/w_j, \qquad i,j = 1,2,...,n \qquad (3.2)$$

Summing up all of j, we obtain

$$\sum_{j=1}^{n} a_{ij} w_j = n w_j, \qquad i = 1,2,...,n \qquad (3.3)$$

In matrix notation, Eq. (3.3) is also equivalent to

$$\mathbf{A}w = nw \qquad (3.4)$$

Table 3.2 Measurement scales of AHP

Intensity of relative importance	Definitions	Explanations
1	Equal importance	Two activities contribute equally to the objective.
3	Weak importance of one over the other	Experience and judgment slightly favor one activity over another.
5	Essential or strong importance	Experience and judgment strongly favor one activity over another.
7	Demonstrated importance	An activity is favored very strongly over another; its dominance is demonstrated in practice.
9	Absolute importance	The evidence favoring one activity over another is of the highest possible order of affirmation.
2, 4, 6, 8	Intermediate values between to adjacent judgments	When compromise is needed.

Source: Saaty (1977, 1980 and 1990).

The vector w is the principal right eigenvector of matrix $\mathbf{A}$ corresponding to the eigenvalue n. If the vector of weights is unknown, then it can be estimated from the pair-wise comparison of matrix $\hat{\mathbf{A}}$ generated by the decision maker by solving for

$$\hat{\mathbf{A}}\hat{w} = n\hat{w} \qquad (3.5)$$

The matrix $\hat{\mathbf{A}}$ contains the pair-wise judgments of the decision maker and approximates matrix $\mathbf{A}$ whose entries are unknown. In Eq. (3.4), λ is an eigenvlaue of $\hat{\mathbf{A}}$ and $\hat{w}$ is the estimated vector of weights. Saaty (1977) uses the largest eigenvalue $\lambda_{\max}$ of $\hat{\mathbf{A}}$ when solving for

$$\hat{\mathbf{A}}\hat{w} = \lambda_{\max}\hat{w} \qquad (3.6)$$

Saaty (1977) has shown that the largest eigenvalue, $\lambda_{\max}$ of a reciprocal matrix $\mathbf{A}$ is always greater than or equal to n. If the pair-wise comparisons do not include any inconsistencies, $\lambda_{\max} = n$. The more consistent the maximum comparisons are, the closer the value of computed λ_{max} to n. A consistency index (**CI**), which measures the inconsistencies of pair-wise comparisons is given in Eq. (3.7).

$$CI = \frac{\lambda_{max} - n}{n - 1} \tag{3.7}$$

A consistency ratio (**CR**) is given by Eq. (3.8).

$$CR = \left(\frac{CI}{RI}\right) \times 100\%, \tag{3.8}$$

where **CI** is the consistency index; **RI** is the random index; and n is the number of columns. The **RI** is the average of the **CI** of a large number of randomly generated matrices, where n is the matrix size. Judgment consistency can be checked by taking the **CR** of **CI** with the appropriate value in Table 3.3.

RI depends on the order of the matrix. **CR** of 10% or less is considered acceptable (Saaty, 1980).

Steps 3–5 are performed for all levels in the hierarchy. Fortunately, there is no need to implement the steps manually. Professional commercial software, Expert Choice, developed by Expert Choice, Inc is available on the market which simplifies the implementation of the AHP's steps and automates many of its computations.

Finally, after determining the weights of totally 66 indicators, the successive process is to aggregate total indicators into the integrated assessment index of tourism global competitiveness, I_{TGC}, as follows:

Table 3.3 Average random consistency (**RI**)

Size of matrix	1	2	3	4	5	6	7	8	9	10
Random Consistency	0.00	0.00	0.58	0.90	1.12	1.24	1.32	1.41	1.45	1.49

Source: Saaty (1977, 1980 and 1990).

$$I_{TGC} = \sum_{i=1}^{66} I_i \times w_i , \tag{3.9}$$

where I_i is the value of the indicator i; w_i is the element in eigenvector $\hat{w}$. Generally, the larger value of I_{TGC} implies higher level of tourism global competitiveness of a destination, and vice versa.

In fact, values of those indicators may be often expressed in different units from any destination. A suitable standardization procedure for any indicator could employ Eqs. (3.10) and (3.11):

$$I_{S,i}^{+} = \frac{I_i^{+} - I_{min}^{+}}{I_{max}^{+} - I_{min}^{+}} \tag{3.10}$$

$$I_{S,i}^{-} = \frac{I_{max}^{-} - I_i^{-}}{I_{max}^{-} - I_{min}^{-}} , \tag{3.11}$$

where $I_{S,i}^{+}$ is the normalized indicator i of type "more is better;" $I_{S,i}^{-}$ is the normalized indicator i of type "less is better."

In that way, the possibility of incorporating different kinds of quantities, with different units of measurement is offered. One of the advantages of the proposed normalization of indicators is the clear compatibility of different indicators, since all indicators are normalized. Then, I_i in Eq. (3.9) are replaced by Eqs. (3.10) and (3.11) to receive eventual tourism competitiveness ranking of a destination among all data-collected destinations.

However, this final competitiveness ranking computation is cost consuming and is beyond the scope of this dissertation. It could be left to the successors in the future.

References

Arrow KJ (1962) The economic implications of learning by doing. The Review of Economic Studies 29:155–173.
Bramwell B, Rawding L (1996) Tourism marketing images of industrial cities. Annals of Tourism Research 23:201–221.

Buhails D (2000) Marketing the competitive destination of the future. Tourism Management 21:97–116.

Chon KS, Mayer KJ (1995) Destination competitiveness models in tourism and their application in Las Vegas. Journal of Tourism Systems and Quality Management 1:227–246.

Clements MA, Georgiou A (1998) The impact of political instability on a fragile tourism product. Tourism Management 19:283–288.

CNN Television News Reports (2001) September 14, October 1, and October 5, 2001.

Crouch GI, Ritchie JRB (1999) Tourism, competitiveness, and societal prosperity. Journal of Business Research 44:137–152.

Crouch GI, Ritchie JRB (2000) The competitive destination: A sustainability perspective. Tourism Management 21:1–7.

Dann GMS (1996) Tourists images of a destination: An alternative analysis. Journal of Travel and Tourism Marketing 5:41–55.

Driscoll A, Lawson R, Niven B (1994) Measuring tourists' destination perceptions. Annals of Tourism Research 21:499–511.

Dwyer L, Forsyth P, Rao P (2000) The price competitiveness of travel and tourism: A comparison of 19 destinations. Tourism Management 21:9–22.

Dwyer L, Forsyth P, Rao P (2002) Destination price competitiveness: Exchange rate changes versus domestic inflation. Journal of Travel Research 40: 328–336.

Echtner CM, Ritchie JRB (1993) The measurement of destination image: An empirical assessment. Journal of Travel Research 31:3–13.

Enright MJ, Newton J (2004) Tourism destination competitiveness: A quantitative approach. Tourism Management 25:777–788.

Enright MJ, Newton J (2005) Determinants of tourism destination competitiveness in Asia Pacific: Comprehensiveness and universality. Journal of Travel Research 43:339–350.

Fakeye PC, Crompton JL (1991) Image differences between prospective, first-time, and repeat visitors to the lower Rio Grande Valley. Journal of Travel Research 30:10–16.

Gallarza MG, Saura IG, García HC (2002) Destination image: Towards a Conceptual Framework. Annals of Tourism Research 29:56–72.

Gearing CE, Swart WW, Var T (1974) Establishing a measure of touristic attractiveness. Journal of Travel Research 12:1–8.

Goodrich JN (2002) September 11, 2001 attack on America: a record of the immediate impacts and reactions in the USA travel and tourism industry. Tourism Management 23:573–580.

Hassan SS (2000) Determinants of market competitiveness in an environmentally sustainable tourism industry. Journal of Travel Research 38:239–245.

Henderson JC (1999) Southeast Asian tourism and the financial crisis: Indonesia and Thailand compared. Current Issues in Tourism 2:294–303.

Hou JS, Lin CH, Morais DB (2005) Antecedents of attachment to a cultural tourism destination: The case of Hakka and non-Hakka Taiwanese visitors to Pei-pu, Taiwan. Journal of Travel Research 44:221–233.

Hu YZ, Ritchie JRB (1993) Measuring destination attractiveness: A contextual approach. Journal of Travel Research 32:25–34.

Huang JH, Min JCH (2002) Earthquake devastation and recovery in tourism: The Taiwan case. Tourism Management 23:145–154.

Krugman P (1979) Increasing returns, monopolistic competition and international trade. Journal of International Economics 9:469–479.

Lucas RE (1988) On the mechanism of economic development. Journal of Monetary Economics 22:3–42.

McCain G, Ray NM (2003) Legacy tourism: The search for personal meaning in heritage travel. Tourism Management 24:713–717.

McKercher B, Chon K (2004) The over-reaction to SARS and the collapse of Asian tourism. Annals of Tourism Research 31:716–719.

Miller G (1956) The magical number of seven plus or minus two: Some limits on our capacity for processing information. Psychological Review 63:81–97.

Murphy P, Pritchard MP, Smith B (2000) The destination product and its impact on traveler perceptions. Tourism Management 21:43–52.

Poon A (1993) Tourism, technology and competitive strategy. CAB International: Wallingford (UK).

Porter ME (1985) Competitive advantages: Creating and sustaining superior performance. The Free Press: New York.

Porter ME (1990) The competitive advantages of nations. The Free Press: New York.

Ritchie JRB (1975) Some critical aspects of measurement theory and practice in travel research. Journal of Travel Research 14:1–10.

Romer P (1990) Endogenous technological change. Journal of Political Economy 98:S71–S102.

Russo AP, van der Borg J (2002) Planning considerations for cultural tourism: a case study of four European cities. Tourism Management 23:631–637.

Saaty TL (1977) A scaling method for priorities in hierarchical structures. Journal of Mathematical Psychology 15:234–281.

Saaty TL (1980) The analytic hierarchy process. McGraw-Hill: New York.

Saaty TL (1990) How to make a decision: The analytic hierarchy process. European Journal of Operational Research 48:9–26.

Schumpeter J (1912) The theory of economic development. Duncker & Humblot: Leipzig. Reprinted in 1934 by Cambridge: Harvard University Press, and added subtitle "An inquiry into profits, capital, interest and the business cycle."

Selby M, Morgan NG (1996) Reconstructing place image: A case study of its role in destination market research. Tourism Management 17:287–294.

Stevens T (1992) Trends in the Attractions Industry. World Travel and Tourism Review 2:177–181.

Wilder-Smith A (2006) The severe acute respiratory syndrome: Impact on travel and tourism. Travel Medicine and Infectious Disease 4:53–60.

Yang XK (1994) Endogenous vs. exogenous comparative advantage and economies of specialization vs. economies of scale. Journal of Economics 60:29–54.

4 Weight of Indicators and Decision Analyses

4.1 AHP Questionnaire Survey Procedure

The printed questionnaire using the factors and structured elements shown in Table 3.1 was prepared in to gather data for the AHP analysis, which is shown in Appendix.

1. The questionnaire interviewers.

The questionnaire was distributed to: (1) scholars or researchers with more than 3 years of research experience in tourism competitiveness; and (2) government officials ho majored in conducting tourism related affairs.

2. Response status.

The survey activity was conducted from 15th January to 10th June, 2007 via regular mail and e-mail approaches. Approximately 2 weeks after the first mailing, the non-respondents were sent a reminder letter, questionnaire and return envelope. Additional reminders were sent by email to non-respondents at 2-week intervals. The respondents were guaranteed confidentiality and were sent the overall averaged results of the survey and the averaged results for their opinions.

The study surveyed 15 scholars/researchers and four government officials. Of these, four respondents were eliminated from analysis due to lack of consistency (CR>0.1). The response status is shown in Table 4.1. And the valid respondents list is available if request.

Table 4.1 Response status of this study

Interviewers	Sending out	Respondents	Effective response
Scholars/Researchers	20	17	15
Government officials	10	6	4
Total	30	23	19

W.-C. Hong, *Competitiveness in the Tourism Sector.* Contributions to Economics,
doi: 10.1007/978-3-7908-2042-3_4, © Physica-Verlag Heidelberg 2008

4.2 Weight of Indicators Analysis

Via pair-wise comparison judgments of AHP and relevant matrices calculation techniques, these hierarchical weights (i.e., principal evaluation dimensions, elements and detail indicators) could be obtained. Notably, the
obtained weights (local priorities) represented the priorities in the associated hierarchy. The results of those obtained weights are shown in the following sections.

4.2.1 Weight Analysis on Principal Evaluation Dimensions

Among the six principal evaluation dimensions, exogenous comparative advantages, endogenous comparative advantages, competitive advantages,
tourism management, domestic environment conditions, and global environment conditions, the analytical results (see Fig. 4.1) showed that exogenous comparative advantages (weight, 49.18%) was the most important factor for enhancing the tourism competitiveness of a destination. Other
important factors are competitive advantage (weight, 17.27%), tourism management (weight, 12.01%), endogenous comparative advantage (weight,
10.62%), and global environment conditions (weight, 6.03%). The least important factor is domestic environment conditions (weight, 4.89%).

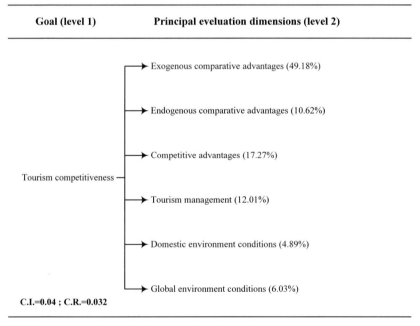

Fig. 4.1 Importance of principal evaluation dimensions

As concluded by Russo and van der Borg (2002), McCain and Ray (2003), and Hou et al. (2005), *exogenous comparative advantages* play a critical role in the composition of the tourism competitiveness. However, in addition to developing these exogenous resources, improving or enhancing destination competitiveness is also important. Additionally, it is important to combine theories and concepts of *competitive advantage* for a more detailed analysis of this issue. As Enright and Newton (2004) indicated, "a destination is competitive if it can attract and satisfy potential tourists, and this competitiveness is determined both by tourism-specific factors and a much wider range of factors that influence the tourism service providers." Conversely, excellent *tourism management* performance also played a key role in enhancing the competitiveness of a destination.

4.2.2 Weight Analysis on Comparative Advantages

The evaluation dimension of exogenous comparative advantages is composed of three elements: *natural resources, cultural/heritage resources* and *capital resources*. The analytical results (see Fig. 4.2) indicate that *cultural/heritage resources* (weight, 46.87%) are the most important element. This element, representing a high rate of *history* (weight, 47.25%), is the most heavily weighted leading indicator. Additionally,

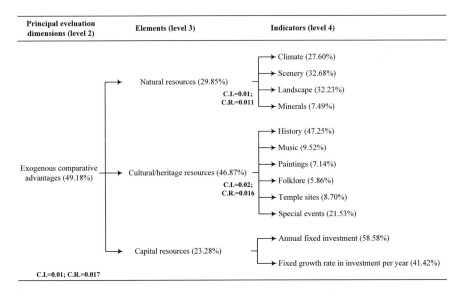

Fig. 4.2 Importance of elements and indicators of exogenous comparative advantages

special events (weight, 21.53%) are another important indicator of enhanced cultural/heritage resources. Secondly, *natural resources* (weight, 29.85%) is the second most significant element in exogenous comparative advantages improvement, and *scenery* (weight, 32.68%) and *landscape* (weight, 32.23%) are selected as the most significant indicators of the natural resources improvement element. Finally, *capital resources* (weight, 23.28%) are the least important in exogenous comparative advantages improvement.

The analytical results indicate that cultural tourism (Russo & van der Borg, 2002) has become a holistic process to provide the source of tourism attractiveness. Thus, local festival celebrations of a specific destination should be based on characteristic folklore, i.e., so-called special events, to help create the principal memorable experiences of a destination for tourists.

The evaluation dimension of endogenous comparative advantages is composed of three elements: *human resources, knowledge resources* and *technological innovation*. The analytical results (see Fig. 4.3) indicate that *human resources* (weight, 66.53%) is the most important element, and this element representing a high rate of *education in commerce* (weight, 47.67%) is the most heavily weighted. Secondly, *knowledge resources* is the second significant element (weight, 20.01%) of endogenous comparative advantage improvement. Any destination should consider expanding

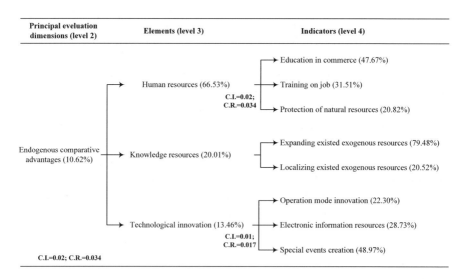

Fig. 4.3 Importance of elements and indicators of endogenous comparative advantages

its existing exogenous resources to enrich its management knowledge. Finally, *technological innovation* (weight, 13.46%) is the least important for improving endogenous comparative advantage; however, *special events creation* is identified as the most significant indicator (weight, 48.97%) for enhancing the technological innovation element.

Based on these analytical results, it is important to implement a series of human resource improvement activities to enhance the endogenous comparative advantages of a destination, through the learning by doing process described by Arrow (1962), the specialization of employees (training on job) described by Yang (1994) and the protection of natural resources. Additionally, as noted by Schumpeter (1912), tourist travel to a destination to receive destination services and associated experiences represents a potential new market important to the tourism industry. In such cases, special events creation becomes more significant in developing countries. Of course, new service mode innovations and novel approaches for providing services are also important issues. Further, knowledge resources should carefully examined by introducing successful operational knowledge to a new destination (Lucas' spillover effect occurs) to expand its existing exogenous resources.

4.2.3 Weight Analysis on Competitive Advantages

The evaluation dimension of competitive advantages is composed of seven elements: infrastructure investments, strategic planning to market ties, maintaining resources, monitoring resource allocations, growth and development, operational performance effectiveness and facilitating resource creation. The analytical results (see Fig. 4.4) show that infrastructure investment (weight, 38.48%) is the most important element for enhancing the competitive advantages of a destination, and the indicator of accessibility designing is the most important weight (weight, 37.94%) in this element. Thus, convenient transit system design for connecting with scheduled flight (arrival and departure) and local transportation systems and accommodation support would be the most important issue for enhancing the competitive advantages of a destination. The second important element is growth and development (weight, 17.08%). Rapid or continued economic growth would attract FDI in key industries then generate market ties (including ethnic ties, business ties, and leisure ties) which would lead to steady tourist flow.

The third important element is *operational performance effectiveness* (weight, 14.95%). One alternative is *one-stop tourism package services*. Its priority is determined by the upper-level weights. As Porter indicated,

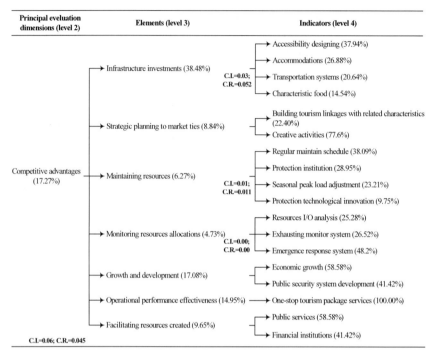

Fig. 4.4 Importance of elements and indicators of competitive advantages

sophisticated domestic tourists and their high level demands are an incentive for delivery of specific services. Thus, integrating total tourism services (pleasure parks, hotels, restaurants, resorts, tourism fruit farms, and so on) of a destination into a selection package could significantly attract tourists.

Facilitating resource creation (weight, 9.65%), *strategic planning to develop market ties* (weight, 8.84%) and *maintaining resources* (weight, 6.27%) are also important elements. Thus, for a destination with limited tourism resources, implementing a regular maintain schedule on a monthly, quarterly or annual basis is particularly important for preserving fragile cultural heritages, buildings, related landscapes and general tourism resources subject to harsh weather conditions. Convenient public services (including sufficient information or more detailing specifics, such as rapid post delivery services, high quality telecommunication, barrier free public environment designing) and financial institutions (including related financial services, such as travel check, currency exchange, money remittance) are also important for improving competitive advantage. The least important element is *monitoring resources allocations* (weight, 4.73%).

4.2.4 Weight Analysis on Tourism Management

The evaluation dimension of tourism management is composed of six elements: *resource stewardship training, marketing, organization and regulations, business or firm integration, information providing,* and *services.* The analytical results (see Fig. 4.5) indicate that *marketing* is the most important element (weight, 23.66%), making the *reasonable pricing policies* indicator the most important weight (weight, 34.20%) in this element. Other important elements include *business or firm integration* (weight, 21.22%), *services* (weight, 17.95%), *organization and regulations* (weight, 15.36%) and *information providing* (weight, 14.5%). Finally, *resource stewardship training* (weight, 7.31%) is the least important for tourism management improvement.

Marketing is the most traditional strategic tool/activity for promoting tourism resources of a destination. The analytical results in this study once again indicated its importance, particularly in special events creation, market tie establishments, pricing policy to adjust the number of tourist visits between seasonal peak period and the slack season and market segment.

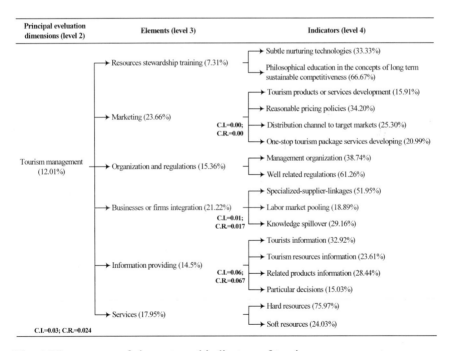

Fig. 4.5 Importance of elements and indicators of tourism management

Furthermore, effective *management organization and regulations* are required for high decision-making quality in promoting the attractiveness of a destination. Effective collaboration projects are also needed. Thus, well defined regulations would also encourage management organizations to engage in strategic planning of tourism development to shape the competitive advantages of a destination with respect to future challenges. Finally, *businesses clusters or firms integration* can bring together many firms that can provide a large enough investment to support specialized suppliers. Meanwhile, it can also create a pooled market for workers with highly specialized skills needed in the tourism industry. As Krugman (1979) suggested, "with the effects of regional agglomeration, trade may be a way of extending the market and allowing exploitation of scale economies."

4.2.5 Weight Analysis on Environment Conditions

The evaluation dimension of domestic environment conditions is composed of two elements: *chance events* and *superstructure changes*. The analytical results (see Fig. 4.6) indicate that *superstructure change* is the most important element (weight, 79.48%) and gives the three indicators *ethic tensions harmonization* (weight, 35.70%), *cultural diversification* (weight, 25.58%), and *political climate changes* (weight, 20.31%) sequential weights for this element. The analytical results indicate that creating a stable political climate and implementing plicy for harmonizing ethnic tensions are important for any destination and can enhance economic development, attract international tourists and encourage tourism development, all of which eventually shape competitiveness. Additionally, providing diversified cultural tourism experiences would also increase attractiveness to potential tourists and shape the unique characteristics of a destination.

Secondly, *chance events* are also a considerable element (weight, 20.52%) for demostic environment conditions. *Spread of disease* (weight, 40.78%) and significant *world financial exchange markets events* (weight, 36.33%) are selected as the significant indicators to affect the domestic environment security and safety considerations. Based on the result, it is also an important issue to construct disease information/announcement networks, to effectively prevent disease transmission in the journey, and slow down the speed of its spread through. Conversely, appropriate financial intervention policy could prevent local financial market from losing change value of its currency, unemployment, rising prices and food shortages, and eventually ensure the tourism industry.

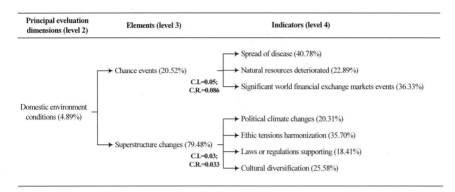

Fig. 4.6 Importance of elements and indicators of domestic environment conditions

The evaluation dimension of global environment conditions is composed of two elements: *accidental events* and *expected events*. The analytical results (see Fig. 4.7) indicate that *accidental events* are more important (weight, 81.73%), and put the most weight on this element. *Terrorist attack* is the leading indicator (weight, 69.10%). Secondly, *expected events* (weight, 18.27%) are also a considerably affect global environment conditions, and *wars* (weight, 79.48%) are selected as the most significant indicator of global environment security and safety.

In tourism competition, stable global environment conditions are needed for more peaceful atmospheres. Thus, based on the above results, any government of a destination should pay more attention to global affairs such as by issuing a democracy/peace communique, promoting humanism and global collaboration in anti-terrorism activities. Additionally, any new tourism destination can employ these measures to enhance the attractiveness of its tourism products and services to potential tourists.

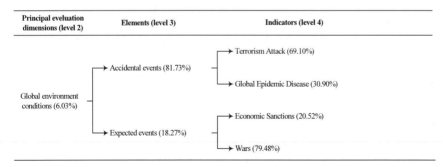

Fig. 4.7 Importance of elements and indicators of global environment conditions

4.3 Statistical Analyses and Feasible Decissions Considerations

To verify the influential effects indicated in Chap. 3 and to make several feasiblity decisions for improving or enhancing the tourism competitiveness of a destination, the AHP questionnaire survey was expanded to include thirteen additional questions. In the revised survey, respondents were asked to evaluate their perception of several items as to their influential effects on RCA, PCA and tourism management. Each of the items was based on the discussion in Chap. 3. Additionally, the respondents were asked to rate these items on a five-point Likert scale. The Likert scale used 1 (one) as "strongly disagree", 2 (two) as "disagree", 3 (three) as "neutral", 4(four) as "agree", and 5 (five) as "strongly agree".

Meanwhile, the reliability and validity of the data collection process was examined. For the reliability issue, because scholars/experts and specific government officials were asked to respond to the questionnaire survey, it is important to consider the internal consistency reliability. Thus, reliability was judged by estimating how well the items reflecting the same construct yielded similar results and how consistent the results were for different items for the same construct within the measure. Many internal consistency measures are possible. In this study, the Cronbach α inter-rater reliability was employed, as shown in Eq. (4.1)

$$\alpha = \frac{k}{k-1}\left(\frac{s_T^2 - \sum_{i=1}^{k} s_i^2}{s_T^2}\right) \tag{4.1}$$

where k is the number of items, s_i^2 is the variance of the ith item and s_T^2 is the variance of the total score formed by summing all the items.

In this study, the Cronbach α had an average of 0.78, which exceeds the minimum acceptable level of 0.70 for exploratory research (Nunnally & Bernstein, 1994).

Similarly, validity refers to the degree to which inferences can legitimately be made from the operationalizations in this study to the theoretical constructs on which those operationalizations were based. Dick and Hagerty (1971) suggested that the maximal value of validity (β) could be calculated by Eq. (4.2),

$$\text{Max } \beta = \sqrt{\alpha} \tag{4.2}$$

In this study, the maximal value of validity (β) was an average of 0.883, which is beyond the minimum acceptable level of 0.50 for exploratory research (Nunnally & Bernstein, 1994).

Using data from each respondent, mean scores and standard deviation on evaluative agreeableness and attitudes toward each item were calculated. Table 4.2 presents these calculation results. Mean scores of all except 5, 8 and 10-1 were higher than the expected value of 3, and these results indicated that most respondents agreed that these 13 items were influential effects among RCA, PCA and tourism management.

1. RCA-Originated Influential Effects

As Table 4.2 indicates, exogenous comparative advantages interaction effects directly enhance competitive advantages, and, in the influential process, effective tourism management play are a catalyst in providing suitable assistance to enhance PCA. However, the effect of endogenous comparative advantages is minimal, according to the the mean score for *Influential Effect* of 5, which is lower than the expected expected value of 3. Thus, RCA-originated influential effects (including exogenous comparative advantages, endogenous comparative advantages and tourism management) are valuable for strategic planning to enhance PCA.

Thus, these findings provide numerous feasible decision making considerations, such as developing special transportation systems for specific climate, scenery, or landscape (e.g., cable railway system for high mountains and virgin forests); employing abundant cultural/heritage resources to hold traditional cultural activities, exhibitions, fairs, expositions, or promoting the regular festivals and ceremonies to attract ethnic tie- and market tie-related visitors (potential tourists); characteristic foods and accommodations can also be inherited from the abundant cultural resources of a destination (e.g., famous historical stories, folklores, or special events). Additionally, stewardships training for natural resources protection, nurturing technology education and establishing novel information systems are also considered (complete soft resources and convenient inter-modal transfer information).

Table   4.2 Mean scores and standard deviations for each influential effect

Influential effects	Mean scores	Standard deviation
Effect 1: Well natural endowments would support to promote infrastructure investments with destination's characteristics.	4.1579	0.6021
Effect 2: Well endowments would support to plan suitable strategies for establishing market ties.	4.2631	0.5620
Effect 3: Well tourism management abilities would help for competitive advantages.	3.6842	0.6710
Effect 4: Well improvable tourism resources would support market ties strategies planning.	3.8421	0.7647
Effect 5: Well human resources would provide effective resources maintaining, protection, and nurturing which directly enhance the sustainability of a destination's PCA.	2.7368	0.8057
Effect 6: Well specified tourism management abilities would play the role of catalyst to enhance competitive advantages.	4.3684	0.4956
Effect 7: Well infrastructure investments would provide impressions to enhance the attractiveness for natura/cultural resources.	4.1579	0.6882
Effect 8: Well strategic planning to market ties could enhance the attractiveness of a specific cultural resource.	2.8947	0.6578
Effect 9-1: Well specified tourism management abilities on emphasizing tourism experiences to enhance its historical popularity and public praise.	3.8421	0.6882
Effect 9-2: Well specified tourism management abilities on increasing the concepts of responsibility and honor for working job would form another famous characteristic tourism resource.	3.4211	0.5073
Effect 10-1: Infrastructure, market ties strategies, and facilitating package services would direct the issues of human resources improvement.	2.5789	0.6925
Effect 10-2: Infrastructure, market ties strategies, and facilitating package services would expand or localize possessed natural resources.	4.0526	0.7375
Effect 10-3: Infrastructure, market ties strategies, and facilitating package services would inspire new special events creation.	4.3158	0.6306

2. PCA-Originated Influential Effects

Conversely, the influential effects of competitive advantage were shown to slightly enhance exogenous comparative advantages (natural, cultural, and heritage resources) according to the mean score of 8 for *Influential Effect 8*, which was lower than the expected value of 3. Similarly, influential effects of competitive advantages also slightly enhance endogenous comparative advantages (human resources improvement) according to the mean score of *Influential Effect 10-1*, which was lower than the expected value of 3. Thus, PCA-originated influential effects (including competitive advantages and tourism management) are valuable for strategic planning to enhance RCA (including exogenous comparative advantages and endogenous comparative advantages).

Influential Effect 8 provides insight into the tourism destination experience received. Attractiveness to potential tourists does not mainly depend on strategic planning tools for developing market ties but on the evolutionary affection of natural, cultural, and heritage resources themselves. Thus, these findings also provide useful decision making considerations, such as infrastructure investment (with high accessibility transportation systems, convenient accommodations services), that can increase the attractiveness of natural, cultural and heritage resources (i.e., exogenous comparative advantages).

Regarding *Influential Effect 10-1*, enhancing the human resource improvement considerations via the following processes, infrastructure designing, market ties strategies planning, and facilitating package services providing. Even human resources play the most important role in the element of endogenous comparative advantages. Hence, it will still be the critical issue in tourism management field. Additionally, via stewardships training for emphasizing profound tourism experiences to enhance its popularity and public praise, and to increase the concepts of responsibility and honor for working job, it also could help to form another famous characteristic tourism resource.

References

Arrow KJ (1962) The economic implications of learning by doing. The Review of Economic Studies 29:155–173.

Dick W, Hagerty N (1971) Topics in measurement: Reliability and validity. McGraw-Hill: New York.

Enright MJ, Newton J (2004) Tourism destination competitiveness: A quantitative approach. Tourism Management 25:777–788.

Hou JS, Lin CH, Morais DB (2005) Antecedents of attachment to a cultural tourism destination: The case of Hakka and non-Hakka Taiwanese visitors to Pei-pu, Taiwan. Journal of Travel Research 44:221–233.

Krugman P (1979) Increasing returns, monopolistic competition and international trade. Journal of International Economics 9:469–479.

McCain G, Ray NM (2003) Legacy tourism: The search for personal meaning in heritage travel. Tourism Management 24:713–717.

Nunnally JC, Bernstein IH (1994) Psychometric theory. McGraw-Hill: New York.

Russo AP, van der Borg J (2002) Planning considerations for cultural tourism: A case study of four European cities. Tourism Management 23:631–637.

Schumpeter J (1912) The theory of economic development. Duncker & Humblot: Leipzig. Reprinted in 1934 by Cambridge: Harvard University Press, and added subtitle "An inquiry into profits, capital, interest and the business cycle."

Yang XK (1994) Endogenous vs. exogenous comparative advantage and economies of specialization vs. economies of scale. Journal of Economics 60:29–54.

5 Conclusions and Future Works

5.1 Conclusions

The elements of tourism competitiveness are multi-dimensional and ex-
tremely complex. The study firstly traced the development of theories of
competitiveness to clarify a suitable research scope of tourism competitiveness. Via extensive review of the relevant literature in international
trade and economics, the meaning and the scope of the term "competitiveness" was defined as "the degree to which a nation can, under free and fair
market conditions, produce goods and services that meet the test of international markets while simultaneously maintaining or expanding the real
incomes of its citizens." It's a principal evolutionary tendency of competitiveness is the so-called Ricardian comparative advantages theory (RCA),
which can be based on the conditions of natural endowments (exogenous
comparative advantages) and the degree of technological change (endogenous comparative advantages). Conversely, in the management-related literature, Porter proposed a new analytic framework for competitive advantage, the so-called Porterian competitive advantage framework (PCA), to
explain the increased trade among countries with similar factorial portfolios rather than by examining trade patterns. By the way, although PCA
has been intensely debated among traditional economists, PCA is undoubtedly an influential and paradigmatic perspective on competitiveness analysis and has been the subject of extensive empirical research in many fields
during the recent 2 decades. The relevant literature review of competitiveness evaluation, including cost-benefit analysis, resource-based views and
IMD-ranking style, was also conducted. The research framework of competitiveness evolutions is proposed as Fig. 1.1.

Second, this study also traced the development of tourism competition
status to construct an appropriate evaluation framework for tourism competitiveness. The fundamental product in tourism is the destination experience; thus, destination competitiveness involves a wide and complex range
of issues. Mainstream research in tourism competitiveness have focused on

W.-C. Hong, *Competitiveness in the Tourism Sector.* Contributions to Economics,
doi: 10.1007/978-3-7908-2042-3_5, © Physica-Verlag Heidelberg 2008

destination image or attractiveness, including natural resources (e.g., climate, scenery, landscape, minerals), cultural/heritage resources (e.g., history, music, paintings, folklore, temple sites, special events) and functional/physical resources (e.g., accommodations, food, transportation, guiding services, and environmental management), tourism services management issues and environment conditions. These factors have a strong bearing on tourist perceptions, which in turn influence their assessment of destination competitiveness. Additionally, a more comprehensive approach proposed by Crouch and Ritchie (1999) considers both the basic elements of comparative advantages and the advanced elements of competitive advantages were also included in the research framework. The research framework of tourism competitive information is proposed as Fig. 1.2.

Third, the detailed discussion in Chap. 3 examined evaluation dimensions, elements and indicators. Sixty-six indicators were verified to evaluate the overall tourism competitiveness performance of a destination: 20 indicators for comparative advantages performance evaluation, 18 indicators for competitive advantages performance evaluation, 17 indicators for tourism management performance evaluation and 11 indicators for environment conditions performance evaluation. Table 3.1 lists the details of the indicators, and Fig. 3.4 presents the evaluation indicators verification procedure.

Fourth, analytic hierarchy process (AHP) was employed to determine the suitable weights of evalution dimensions, elements and indicators. The analytical results (Fig. 4.1) reveal that *exogenous comparative advantages* (weight, 49.18%) are the most important factor for enhancing the tourism competitiveness of a destination. Other important factors are *competitive advantages* (weight, 17.27%), *tourism management* (weight, 12.01%), *endogenous comparative advantages* (weight, 10.62%) and *global environment conditions* (weight, 6.03%). The least important factor is *domestic environment conditions* (weight, 4.89%).

1. For exogenous comparative advantages (Fig. 4.2), *cultural/heritage resources* (weight, 46.87%) is the most important element, and the most heavily weighted indicator is *history* (weight, 47.25%). *Natural resources* (weight, 29.85%) are the second significant element, and *capital resources* (weight, 23.28%) are the least important for exogenous comparative advantages improvement.
2. For endogenous comparative advantages (Fig. 4.3), *human resources* is the most important element (weight, 66.53%), and its most heavily weighted indicator is *education in commerce* (weight, 47.67%). *Knowledge resources* are the second most significant element

(weight, 20.01%), and *technological innovation* (weight, 13.46%) is the least important for improving endogenous comparative advantage.

3. For competitive advantages (Fig. 4.4), *infrastructure investment* is the most important element (weight, 38.48%), and its most heavily weighted indicator is *accessibility designing* (weight, 37.94%). *Growth and development* is the second most significant element (weight, 17.08%), and *operational performance effectiveness* is the third most important element (weight, 14.95%) for improving competitive advantage. *Facilitating resource creation* (weight, 9.65%), *strategic planning to develop market ties* (weight, 8.84%) and *maintaining resources* (weight, 6.27%) are also important elements. The least important element is *monitoring resource allocations* (weight, 4.73%).

4. For tourism management (Fig. 4.5), *marketing* is the most important element (weight, 23.66%), and its most heavily weighted indicator is *reasonable pricing policies* (weight, 34.20%). The second important elements are *business or firms integration* (weight, 21.22%), *services* (weight, 17.95%), *organization and regulations* (weight, 15.36%) and *information providing* (weight, 14.5%). Finally, *resource stewardship training* (weight, 7.31%) is the least important for improving tourism management.

5. For domestic environment conditions (Fig. 4.6), *superstructure change* is the most important element (weight, 79.48%), and three indicators, *ethic tensions harmonization* (weight, 35.70%), *cultural diversification* (weight, 25.58%), and *political climate changes* (weight, 20.31%) are sequentially weighted in this element. *Chance events* are also a considerable element (weight, 20.52%) for domestic environment conditions. *Spread of disease* (weight, 40.78%) and significant *world financial exchange markets events* (weight, 36.33%) are significant indicators affecting the domestic environment security and safety considerations.

6. For global environment conditions (Fig. 4.7), *accidental events* are the most important element (weight, 81.73%), and the most important indicator is *terrorism attack* (weight, 69.10%). *Expected events* is also a considerable element (weight, 18.27%) in global environment conditions, and *wars* is identified as the most significant indicator (weight, 79.48%) affecting domestic environment security and safety considerations.

Eventually, statistical analyses were conducted to verify the influential effects among RCA, PCA and tourism management. Those calculation results (Table 4.2) indicate that exogenous comparative advantages influential effects directly enhance competitive advantages, and, in the influential process, effective tourism management also could play a vital role in providing suitable assistance to enhance PCA. However, the influential effects of endogenous comparative advantages are negative, as indicated by the mean score of *Influential Effect 5* being lower than the expected expected value 3. Additionally, these statistical analyses results also indicate that competitive advantages of influential effects slightly enhance exogenous comparative advantages (natural, cultural, and heritage resources) due to the mean score of *Influential Effect 8* being lower than the expected expected value of 3. Similarly, the influential effects of competitive advantages also slightly enhance endogenous comparative advantages (human resources improvement). The mean score of *Influential Effect 10-1* is lower than the expected expected value of 3.

5.2 Future Works

The work presented in this dissertation can be extended in many ways to many competitiveness research topics. Here, further areas of research are suggested.

1. Human resources is still an important issue in tourism competitiveness improvement. Human resources enhancement is only minimally affected by competitive advantages activities such as infrastructure, market ties strategies and facilitating package services. Thus, identifying suitable modals or approaches to providing training on job, protection of natural resources and tourism-related education is needed to maintain the competitiveness of a destination.
2. Adjusting evaluation indicators. Due to the dynamics of competitive status in tourism related industries, it is necessary to adjust evaluation indicators in some specific research period.
3. The proposed evaluation framework can also be generalized for application to competitiveness evaluation. An example is agricultural competitiveness evaluation.

Reference

Crouch GI, Ritchie JRB (1999) Tourism, competitiveness, and societal prosperity. Journal of Business Research 44:137–152.

Appendix

AHP Expert Questionnaire

Dear Researcher,
Enclosed please find out the AHP (Analytic Hierarchy Process) Expert Questionnaire regarding the "Evaluation of Tourism Industry Competitiveness." The research project devotes to construct a suitable evaluation structure and its associate indices to understand the compositions of tourism competitiveness and how it would be evaluated. Finally, it is expected to provide policy suggestions to modify or improve the tourism competition edge for governors.

Please fill out the following questionnaire by any available approach, and send back to us directly via regular mail, e-mail, or fax for your convenience. Your kindly attention and prompt response are appreciated and are valuable to us.

Yours sincerely,

Wei-Chiang Hong
Ph.D. Candidate
School of Management
Da Yeh University
112, Shan-Jiau Rd., Da-Tsuen, Changhua, 51505, Taiwan
E-mail: d9230006@mail.oit.edu.tw

1 Instruction for Answering Questions

While answering each question, you should pay attention on the importance comparison between two selected criteria. The numbers of each pair-wise comparison question indicated the preference intensity of your option expressing.

For example, if two criteria are of "**equal**" importance, a value of "**1**" is given in the comparison, while a "**9**" indicates an "**Absolute importance**" of one criterion over the other. Additionally, those intermediate values (e.g., "**2**", "**4**", "**6**", and "**8**") imply intermediate values between adjacent judgments, such as "**8**" implies the compromising important position between "**Demonstrated importance**" and "**Absolute importance**". The following table shows the measurement scale.

Intensity of relative importance	Definitions	Explanations
1	Equal importance	Two activities contribute equally to the objective.
3	Weak importance of one over the other	Experience and judgment slightly favor one activity over another.
5	Essential or strong importance	Experience and judgment strongly favor one activity over another.
7	Demonstrated importance	An activity is favored very strongly over another; its dominance is demonstrated in practice.
9	Absolute importance	The evidence favoring one activity over another is of the highest possible order of affirmation.
2, 4, 6, 8	Intermediate values between to adjacent judgments	When compromise is needed.

Example One

Endogenous Comparative advantages	9	7	5	3	1	3	5	7	9	Competitive advantages
	☐	☐	☐	☐	☐	☐	■	☐	☐	

Example Two

Knowledge resources	9	7	5	3	1	3	5	7	9	Human resources
	☐	☐	☐	☐	■	☐	☐	☐	☐	

The result of Example one indicated that, for a selected decision maker, a "**strong importance**" of the criterion "Competitive advantages" over the other criterion "(Endogenous) Comparative advantages."

The result of Example two indicated that, for a selected decision maker, a "**Equal importance**" of the criterion "**Knowledge resources**" over the other criterion "**Human resources**."

2 The Evaluation Structure of Tourism Industry Competitiveness

This study had summarized the large number of inspirations from economists' and management's perspectives to provide a more comprehensive tourism global competitiveness evaluation model. In this proposed model, those verified indicators are primarily classified into four dimensions, namely **Exogenous Comparative Advantages**, **Endogenous Comparative Advantages**, **Competitive Advantages**, and **Tourism Management**. Secondly, other two dimensions of those verified indicators are regarding environmental considerations, namely **Domestic Environment Conditions** and **Global Environment Conditions**, to provide more generalized perspective and consistent comparison between countries (and between industries) of the tourism sector. Thus, totally, **66** indicators are verified to evaluate the overall tourism competitiveness performance of a destination; **12** indicators for **Exogenous Comparative Advantages** performance evaluation; **8** indicators for **Endogenous Comparative Advantages** performance evaluation; **18** indicators for **Competitive Advantages** performance evaluation; **17** indicators for **Tourism Management** performance evaluation; **7** indicators for **Domestic Environment Conditions** performance evaluation; and **4** indicators for **Global Environment Conditions** performance evaluation; details of total verified indicators are listed in the following table.

Goal	Evaluation dimensions		Detailing indicators
Tourism competitiveness evaluation model	(Exogenous) Comparative advantages	Natural resources	(1) Climate (2) Scenery (3) Landscape (4) Minerals
		Cultural/heritage resources	(5) History (6) Music (7) Paintings (8) Folklore (9) Temple sites (10) Special events
		Capital resources	(11) Annual fixed investment (12) Fixed growth rate in investment per year
	(Endogenous) Comparative advantages	Human resources	(13) Education in commerce (14) Training on job (15) Protection of natural resources
		Knowledge resources	(16) Expanding existed exogenous resources (17) Localizing existed exogenous resources
		Technological innovation	(18) Operation mode innovation (19) Electronic information resources (20) Special events creation
	Competitive advantages	Infrastructure investments	(21) Accessibility designing (22) Accommodations (23) Transportation systems (24) Characteristic food
		Strategic planning to market ties	(25) Building tourism linkages with related characteristics (26) Creative activities
		Maintaining resources	(27) Regular maintain schedule (28) Protection institution (29) Seasonal peak load adjustment (30) Protection technological innovation
		Monitoring resources allocations	(31) Resources I/O analysis (32) Exhausting monitor system (33) Emergence response system
		Growth and development	(34) Economic growth (35) Public security system development

Goal	Evaluation dimensions		Detailing indicators
Tourism competitiveness evaluation model	(Exogenous) Comparative advantages	Operational performance effectiveness	(36) One-stop tourism package services
		Facilitating resources created	(37) Public services (38) Financial institutions
		Resources stewardship training	(39) Subtle nurturing technologies (40) Philosophical education in the concepts of long term sustainable competitiveness
		Marketing	(41) Tourism products or services development (42) Reasonable pricing policies (43) Distribution channel to target markets (44) One-stop tourism package services developing
		Organization and regulations	(45) Management organization (46) Well related regulations
		Businesses or firms integration	(47) Specialized-supplier-linkages (48) Labor market pooling (49) Knowledge spillover
		Information providing	(50) Tourists information (51) Tourism resources information (52) Related products information (53) Particular decisions
		Services	(54) Hard resources (55) Soft resources
	(Domestic) Environment conditions	Chance events	(56) Spread of disease (57) Natural resources deteriorated (58) Significant world financial exchange markets events
		Superstructure changes	(59) Political climate changes (60) Ethic tensions harmonization (61) Laws or regulations supporting (62) Cultural diversification
	(Global) Environment conditions	Accidental events	(63) Terrorism Attack (64) Global Epidemic Disease
		Expected events	(65) Economic Sanctions (66) Wars

3 Questionnaire Contents

3.1 Six Principal Evaluation Dimensions

Left dimension	9		7		5		3		1		3		5		7		9	Right dimension
Exogenous Comparative advantages	☐	☐	☐	☐	☐	☐	☐	☐	☐	☐	☐	☐	☐	☐	☐	☐	☐	Endogenous Comparative advantages
Exogenous Comparative advantages	☐	☐	☐	☐	☐	☐	☐	☐	☐	☐	☐	☐	☐	☐	☐	☐	☐	Competitive advantages
Exogenous Comparative advantages	☐	☐	☐	☐	☐	☐	☐	☐	☐	☐	☐	☐	☐	☐	☐	☐	☐	Tourism management
Exogenous Comparative advantages	☐	☐	☐	☐	☐	☐	☐	☐	☐	☐	☐	☐	☐	☐	☐	☐	☐	Domestic Environment conditions
Exogenous Comparative advantages	☐	☐	☐	☐	☐	☐	☐	☐	☐	☐	☐	☐	☐	☐	☐	☐	☐	Global Environment conditions
Endogenous Comparative advantages	☐	☐	☐	☐	☐	☐	☐	☐	☐	☐	☐	☐	☐	☐	☐	☐	☐	Competitive advantages
Endogenous Comparative advantages	☐	☐	☐	☐	☐	☐	☐	☐	☐	☐	☐	☐	☐	☐	☐	☐	☐	Tourism management

	9	7	5	3	1	3	5	7	9	
Endogenous Comparative advantages	☐	☐	☐	☐	☐	☐	☐	☐	☐	Domestic Environment conditions
Endogenous Comparative advantages	☐	☐	☐	☐	☐	☐	☐	☐	☐	Global Environment conditions
Competitive advantages	☐	☐	☐	☐	☐	☐	☐	☐	☐	Tourism management
Competitive advantages	☐	☐	☐	☐	☐	☐	☐	☐	☐	Domestic Environment conditions
Competitive advantages	☐	☐	☐	☐	☐	☐	☐	☐	☐	Global Environment conditions
Tourism management	☐	☐	☐	☐	☐	☐	☐	☐	☐	Domestic Environment conditions
Tourism management	☐	☐	☐	☐	☐	☐	☐	☐	☐	Global Environment conditions
Domestic Environment conditions	☐	☐	☐	☐	☐	☐	☐	☐	☐	Global Environment conditions

3.2 Evaluation Elements

3.2.1 Exogenous Comparative Advantages

	9	7	5	3	1	3	5	7	9	
Natural resources	☐	☐	☐	☐	☐	☐	☐	☐	☐	Cultural/heritage resources
Natural resources	☐	☐	☐	☐	☐	☐	☐	☐	☐	Capital resources
Cultural/heritage resources	☐	☐	☐	☐	☐	☐	☐	☐	☐	Capital resources

3.2.2 Endogenous Comparative Advantages

	9	7	5	3	1	3	5	7	9	
Human resources	☐	☐	☐	☐	☐	☐	☐	☐	☐	Knowledge resources
Human resources	☐	☐	☐	☐	☐	☐	☐	☐	☐	Technological innovation
Knowledge resources	☐	☐	☐	☐	☐	☐	☐	☐	☐	Technological innovation

3.2.3 Competitive Advantages

	9	7	5	3	1	3	5	7	9	
Infrastructure investments	☐	☐	☐	☐	☐	☐	☐	☐	☐	Strategic planning to market ties
Infrastructure investments	☐	☐	☐	☐	☐	☐	☐	☐	☐	Maintaining resources
Infrastructure investments	☐	☐	☐	☐	☐	☐	☐	☐	☐	Monitoring resources allocations
Infrastructure investments	☐	☐	☐	☐	☐	☐	☐	☐	☐	Growth and development
Infrastructure investments	☐	☐	☐	☐	☐	☐	☐	☐	☐	Operational performance effectiveness
Infrastructure investments	☐	☐	☐	☐	☐	☐	☐	☐	☐	Facilitating resources created
Infrastructure investments	☐	☐	☐	☐	☐	☐	☐	☐	☐	Maintaining resources
Strategic planning to market ties	☐	☐	☐	☐	☐	☐	☐	☐	☐	Monitoring resources allocations
Strategic planning to market ties	☐	☐	☐	☐	☐	☐	☐	☐	☐	Growth and development
Strategic planning to market ties	☐	☐	☐	☐	☐	☐	☐	☐	☐	Operational performance effectiveness

	Facilitating resources created	Monitoring resources allocations	Growth and development	Operational performance effectiveness	Facilitating resources created	Growth and development	Operational performance effectiveness	Facilitating resources created	Operational performance effectiveness	Facilitating resources created	Facilitating resources created
Strategic planning to market ties	☐	☐	☐	☐	☐	☐	☐	☐	☐	☐	☐
Maintaining resources	☐	☐	☐	☐	☐	☐	☐	☐	☐	☐	☐
Maintaining resources	☐	☐	☐	☐	☐	☐	☐	☐	☐	☐	☐
Maintaining resources	☐	☐	☐	☐	☐	☐	☐	☐	☐	☐	☐
Maintaining resources	☐	☐	☐	☐	☐	☐	☐	☐	☐	☐	☐
Monitoring resources allocations	☐	☐	☐	☐	☐	☐	☐	☐	☐	☐	☐
Monitoring resources allocations	☐	☐	☐	☐	☐	☐	☐	☐	☐	☐	☐
Monitoring resources allocations	☐	☐	☐	☐	☐	☐	☐	☐	☐	☐	☐
Growth and development	☐	☐	☐	☐	☐	☐	☐	☐	☐	☐	☐
Growth and development	☐	☐	☐	☐	☐	☐	☐	☐	☐	☐	☐
Operational performance effectiveness	☐	☐	☐	☐	☐	☐	☐	☐	☐	☐	☐

3.2.4 Tourism Management

	9	7	5	3	1	3	5	7	9	
Resources stewardship training	☐	☐	☐	☐	☐	☐	☐	☐	☐	Marketing
Resources stewardship training	☐	☐	☐	☐	☐	☐	☐	☐	☐	Organization and regulations
Resources stewardship training	☐	☐	☐	☐	☐	☐	☐	☐	☐	Businesses or firms integration
Resources stewardship training	☐	☐	☐	☐	☐	☐	☐	☐	☐	Information providing
Resources stewardship training	☐	☐	☐	☐	☐	☐	☐	☐	☐	Services
Marketing	☐	☐	☐	☐	☐	☐	☐	☐	☐	Organization and regulations
Marketing	☐	☐	☐	☐	☐	☐	☐	☐	☐	Businesses or firms integration
Marketing	☐	☐	☐	☐	☐	☐	☐	☐	☐	Information providing
Marketing	☐	☐	☐	☐	☐	☐	☐	☐	☐	Services
Organization and regulations	☐	☐	☐	☐	☐	☐	☐	☐	☐	Businesses or firms integration

Organization and regulations	☐	☐	☐	☐	☐	☐	☐	☐	☐	☐	Information providing
Organization and regulations	☐	☐	☐	☐	☐	☐	☐	☐	☐	☐	Services
Businesses or firms integration	☐	☐	☐	☐	☐	☐	☐	☐	☐	☐	Information providing
Businesses or firms integration	☐	☐	☐	☐	☐	☐	☐	☐	☐	☐	Services
Information providing	☐	☐	☐	☐	☐	☐	☐	☐	☐	☐	Services

3.2.5 Domestic Environment Conditions

	9	7	5	3	1	3	5	7	9	
Chance events	☐	☐	☐	☐	☐	☐	☐	☐	☐	Super- structure changes

3.2.6 Global Environment Conditions

	9	7	5	3	1	3	5	7	9	
Accidental events	☐	☐	☐	☐	☐	☐	☐	☐	☐	Expected events

3.3 Evaluation Indicators

3.3.1 Natural Resources

	9	7	5	3	1	3	5	7	9	
Climate	☐	☐	☐	☐	☐	☐	☐	☐	☐	Scenery
Climate	☐	☐	☐	☐	☐	☐	☐	☐	☐	Landscape
Climate	☐	☐	☐	☐	☐	☐	☐	☐	☐	Minerals
Scenery	☐	☐	☐	☐	☐	☐	☐	☐	☐	Landscape
Scenery	☐	☐	☐	☐	☐	☐	☐	☐	☐	Minerals
Landscape	☐	☐	☐	☐	☐	☐	☐	☐	☐	Minerals

3.3.2 Cultural/Heritage Resources

	9	7	5	3	1	3	5	7	9	
History	☐	☐	☐	☐	☐	☐	☐	☐	☐	Music
History	☐	☐	☐	☐	☐	☐	☐	☐	☐	Paintings
History	☐	☐	☐	☐	☐	☐	☐	☐	☐	Folklore
History	☐	☐	☐	☐	☐	☐	☐	☐	☐	Temple sites
History	☐	☐	☐	☐	☐	☐	☐	☐	☐	Special events
Music	☐	☐	☐	☐	☐	☐	☐	☐	☐	Paintings
Music	☐	☐	☐	☐	☐	☐	☐	☐	☐	Folklore
Music	☐	☐	☐	☐	☐	☐	☐	☐	☐	Temple sites

Music	☐	☐	☐	☐	☐	☐	☐	☐	Special events
Paintings	☐	☐	☐	☐	☐	☐	☐	☐	Folklore
Paintings	☐	☐	☐	☐	☐	☐	☐	☐	Temple sites
Paintings	☐	☐	☐	☐	☐	☐	☐	☐	Special events
Folklore	☐	☐	☐	☐	☐	☐	☐	☐	Temple sites
Folklore	☐	☐	☐	☐	☐	☐	☐	☐	Special events
Temple sites	☐	☐	☐	☐	☐	☐	☐	☐	Special events
	☐	☐	☐	☐	☐	☐	☐	☐	Special events

3.3.3 Capital Resources

	9	7	5	3	1	3	5	7	9	
Annual fixed investment	☐	☐	☐	☐	☐	☐	☐	☐	☐	Fixed growth rate in investment per year

3.3.4 Human Resources

	9	7	5	3	1	3	5	7	9	
Education in commerce	☐	☐	☐	☐	☐	☐	☐	☐	☐	Training on job
Education in commerce	☐	☐	☐	☐	☐	☐	☐	☐	☐	Protection of natural resources
Training on job	☐	☐	☐	☐	☐	☐	☐	☐	☐	Protection of natural resources

3.3.5 Knowledge Resources

	9	7	5	3	1	3	5	7	9	
Expanding existed exogenous resources	☐	☐	☐	☐	☐	☐	☐	☐	☐	Localizing existed exogenous resources

3.3.6 Technological Innovation

	9	7	5	3	1	3	5	7	9	
Operation mode innovation	☐	☐	☐	☐	☐	☐	☐	☐	☐	Electronic information resources
Operation mode innovation	☐	☐	☐	☐	☐	☐	☐	☐	☐	Special events creation
Electronic information resources	☐	☐	☐	☐	☐	☐	☐	☐	☐	Special events creation

3.3.7 Infrastructure Investments

	9	7	5	3	1	3	5	7	9	
Accessibility designing	☐	☐	☐	☐	☐	☐	☐	☐	☐	Accommodations
Accessibility designing	☐	☐	☐	☐	☐	☐	☐	☐	☐	Transportation systems
Accessibility designing	☐	☐	☐	☐	☐	☐	☐	☐	☐	Characteristic food
Accommodations	☐	☐	☐	☐	☐	☐	☐	☐	☐	Transportation systems
Accommodations	☐	☐	☐	☐	☐	☐	☐	☐	☐	Characteristic food
Transportation systems	☐	☐	☐	☐	☐	☐	☐	☐	☐	Characteristic food

3.3.8 Strategic Planning to Market Ties

	9	7	5	3	1	3	5	7	9	
Building tourism linkages with related characteristics	☐	☐	☐	☐	☐	☐	☐	☐	☐	Creative activities

3.3.9 Maintaining Resources

Left	9	7	5	3	1	3	5	7	9	Right
Regular maintain schedule	☐	☐	☐	☐	☐	☐	☐	☐	☐	Protection institution
Regular maintain schedule	☐	☐	☐	☐	☐	☐	☐	☐	☐	Seasonal peak load adjustment
Regular maintain schedule	☐	☐	☐	☐	☐	☐	☐	☐	☐	Protection technological innovation
Protection institution	☐	☐	☐	☐	☐	☐	☐	☐	☐	Seasonal peak load adjustment
Protection institution	☐	☐	☐	☐	☐	☐	☐	☐	☐	Protection technological innovation
Seasonal peak load adjustment	☐	☐	☐	☐	☐	☐	☐	☐	☐	Protection technological innovation

3.3.10 Monitoring Resources Allocations

Left	9	7	5	3	1	3	5	7	9	Right
Resources I/O analysis	☐	☐	☐	☐	☐	☐	☐	☐	☐	Exhausting monitor system
Resources I/O analysis	☐	☐	☐	☐	☐	☐	☐	☐	☐	Emergence response system
Exhausting monitor system	☐	☐	☐	☐	☐	☐	☐	☐	☐	Emergence response system

3.3.11 Growth and Development

	9	7	5	3	1	3	5	7	9	
Economic growth	☐	☐	☐	☐	☐	☐	☐	☐	☐	Public security system development

3.3.12 Facilitating Resources Created

	9	7	5	3	1	3	5	7	9	
Public services	☐	☐	☐	☐	☐	☐	☐	☐	☐	Financial institutions

3.3.13 Resources Stewardship Training

	9	7	5	3	1	3	5	7	9	
Subtle nurturing technologies	☐	☐	☐	☐	☐	☐	☐	☐	☐	Philosophical education in the concepts of long term sustainable competitiveness

3.3.14 Marketing

Left item	9	7	5	3	1	3	5	7	9	Right item
Tourism products or services development	☐	☐	☐	☐	☐	☐	☐	☐	☐	Reasonable pricing policies
Tourism products or services development	☐	☐	☐	☐	☐	☐	☐	☐	☐	Distribution channel to target markets
Tourism products or services development	☐	☐	☐	☐	☐	☐	☐	☐	☐	One-stop tourism package services developing
Reasonable pricing policies	☐	☐	☐	☐	☐	☐	☐	☐	☐	Distribution channel to target markets
Reasonable pricing policies	☐	☐	☐	☐	☐	☐	☐	☐	☐	One-stop tourism package services developing
Distribution channel to target markets	☐	☐	☐	☐	☐	☐	☐	☐	☐	One-stop tourism package services developing

3.3.15 Organization and Regulations

	9	7	5	3	1	3	5	7	9	
Management organization	☐	☐	☐	☐	☐	☐	☐	☐	☐	Well related regulations

3.3.16 Businesses or Firms Integration

	9	7	5	3	1	3	5	7	9	
Specialized-supplier-linkages	☐	☐	☐	☐	☐	☐	☐	☐	☐	Labor market pooling
Specialized-supplier-linkages	☐	☐	☐	☐	☐	☐	☐	☐	☐	Knowledge spillover
Labor market pooling	☐	☐	☐	☐	☐	☐	☐	☐	☐	Knowledge spillover

3.3.17 Information Providing

Left	9	7	5	3	1	3	5	7	9	Right
Tourists information	☐	☐	☐	☐	☐	☐	☐	☐	☐	Tourism resources information
Tourists information	☐	☐	☐	☐	☐	☐	☐	☐	☐	Related products information
Tourists information	☐	☐	☐	☐	☐	☐	☐	☐	☐	Particular decisions
Tourism resources information	☐	☐	☐	☐	☐	☐	☐	☐	☐	Related products information
Tourism resources information	☐	☐	☐	☐	☐	☐	☐	☐	☐	Particular decisions
Related products information	☐	☐	☐	☐	☐	☐	☐	☐	☐	Particular decisions

3.3.18 Services

Left	9	7	5	3	1	3	5	7	9	Right
Hard resources	☐	☐	☐	☐	☐	☐	☐	☐	☐	Soft resources

3.3.19 Chance Events

	9	7	5	3	1	3	5	7	9	
Spread of disease	☐	☐	☐	☐	☐	☐	☐	☐	☐	Natural resources deteriorated
Spread of disease	☐	☐	☐	☐	☐	☐	☐	☐	☐	Significant world financial exchange markets events
Natural resources deteriorated	☐	☐	☐	☐	☐	☐	☐	☐	☐	Significant world financial exchange markets events

3.3.20 Superstructure Changes

	9	7	5	3	1	3	5	7	9	
Political climate changes	☐	☐	☐	☐	☐	☐	☐	☐	☐	Ethic tensions harmonization
Political climate changes	☐	☐	☐	☐	☐	☐	☐	☐	☐	Laws or regulations supporting
Political climate changes	☐	☐	☐	☐	☐	☐	☐	☐	☐	Cultural diversification
Ethic tensions harmonization	☐	☐	☐	☐	☐	☐	☐	☐	☐	Laws or regulations supporting
Ethic tensions harmonization	☐	☐	☐	☐	☐	☐	☐	☐	☐	Cultural diversification
Laws or regulations supporting	☐	☐	☐	☐	☐	☐	☐	☐	☐	Cultural diversification

3.3.21 Accidental Events

Terrorism Attack 9 ☐ 7 ☐ 5 ☐ 3 ☐ 1 ☐ ☐ 3 ☐ 5 ☐ 7 ☐ 9 ☐ Global Epidemic Disease

3.3.22 Expected Events

Economic Sanctions 9 ☐ 7 ☐ 5 ☐ 3 ☐ 1 ☐ ☐ 3 ☐ 5 ☐ 7 ☐ 9 ☐ Wars

3.4 Interaction Effects

The so-called interaction effects could be composed of two sections, based on the causal origins of interaction, namely RCA(Ricardian comparative advantages)-originated and PCA(Porter's competitive advantages)-originated, respectively.

RCA-originated interaction effects mainly indicate that exogenous comparative advantages and endogenous comparative advantages would provide robust support for strategic consideration to enhance PCA. In the meanwhile, tourism management, the third parts of internal indicators determining tourism competitiveness of a destination, would play the role of catalyst to assist implementation of RCA-originated interaction effects, as illustrated in Fig. A.1.

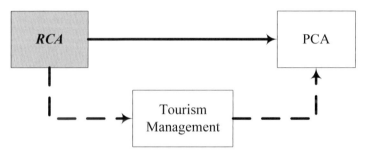

Fig. A.1 RCA-originated interaction effects

PCA-originated interaction effects mainly indicate that Porter's competitive advantages would provide strategic supports for value-added creation to enhance RCA. Similarly, tourism management would also play the role of catalyst to assist implementation of PCA-originated interaction effects, as illustrated in Fig. A.2.

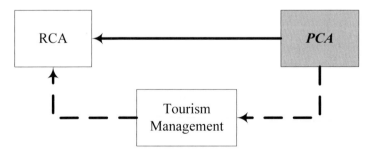

Fig. A.2 PCA-originated interaction effects

1. Well "**Natural resources**" endowments would provide useful supports to promote "**Infrastructure investments**" full with target destination's characteristics. Did you agree with this proposition?
    □ (5)Very agree; □ (4)Agree; □ (3)Neutral; □ (2)Disagree; □ (1)Very disagree

2. Well "**Natural resources**" endowments would also provide useful supports to plan suitable "**Strategies for establishing market ties**". Did you agree with this proposition? □ (5)Very agree; □ (4)Agree; □ (3)Neutral; □ (2)Disagree; □ (1)Very disagree

3. Well "**Tourism management**" abilities (e.g., marketing strategies planning, stewardships training, resources transmitting and maintaining) would simultaneously provide useful, direct, prompt, and suitable helps to "**Competitive advantages**". Did you agree with this proposition? □ (5)Very agree; □ (4)Agree; □ (3)Neutral; □ (2)Disagree; □ (1)Very disagree

4. Well improvable "**Endogenous comparative advantages**" (e.g., special events creation, expanding possessed exogenous resources) would provide useful supports to "**Strategies for establishing market ties**". Did you agree with this proposition? □ (5)Very agree; □ (4)Agree; □ (3)Neutral; □ (2)Disagree; □ (1)Very disagree

5. Well "**Human resources**" (e.g., well education, training courses) would provide effective "**Maintaining resources**" (e.g., resources protection, nurturing) to directly enhance the sustainability of a destination's competitive advantages. Did you agree with this proposition? □ (5)Very agree; □ (4)Agree; □ (3)Neutral; □ (2)Disagree; □ (1)Very disagree

6. Well specified "**Tourism management**" abilities (e.g., special events creation strategies, professional stewardships training for natural resources protections and nurturing, novel information systems) would play the role of catalyst to "**Competitive advantages**". Did you agree with this proposition? □ (5)Very agree; □ (4)Agree; □ (3)Neutral; □ (2)Disagree; □ (1)Very disagree

7. Well "**Infrastructure investments**" (e.g., high accessibility transportation systems, convenient accommodations services) would provide impressions to enhance the attractiveness for "**Natural resources**". Did you agree with this proposition? □ (5)Very agree; □ (4)Agree; □ (3)Neutral; □ (2)Disagree; □ (1)Very disagree

8. Well **"Strategic planning to market ties"** (e.g., linking up the provenances of characteristic foods and activities creation with famous historical stories, folklores, or special events) could enhance the attractiveness of a specific **"Cultural resource"**. Did you agree with this proposition? ☐ (5)Very agree; ☐ (4)Agree; ☐ (3)Neutral; ☐ (2)Disagree; ☐ (1)Very disagree

9. Well specified **"Tourism management"** abilities on emphasizing tourism experiences (e.g., high accessibility transportation systems, convenient accommodations services, characteristic foods, and activities creation) to enhance its **"Cultural/heritage resources"** (e.g. historical popularity, public praise). Did you agree with this proposition? ☐ (5)Very agree; ☐ (4)Agree; ☐ (3)Neutral; ☐ (2)Disagree; ☐ (1)Very disagree

10. Well specified **"Tourism management"** abilities on increasing the concepts of responsibility and honor for working job to form another famous **"Characteristic tourism resource"**. Did you agree with this proposition? ☐ (5)Very agree; ☐ (4)Agree; ☐ (3)Neutral; ☐ (2)Disagree; ☐ (1)Very disagree

11. Well **"Infrastructure"** would direct the issues of **"Human resources"** improvement considerations. Did you agree with this proposition? ☐ (5)Very agree; ☐ (4)Agree; ☐ (3)Neutral; ☐ (2)Disagree; ☐ (1)Very disagree

12. Well **"Infrastructure"** would provide more spread insights to **"Localize possessed natural resources"**. Did you agree with this proposition? ☐ (5)Very agree; ☐ (4)Agree; ☐ (3)Neutral; ☐ (2)Disagree; ☐ (1)Very disagree

13. Well **"Infrastructure"** would also inspire new direction for **"Special events creation"**. Did you agree with this proposition? ☐ (5)Very agree; ☐ (4)Agree; ☐ (3)Neutral; ☐ (2)Disagree; ☐ (1)Very disagree

Printing: Krips bv, Meppel, The Netherlands
Binding: Stürtz, Würzburg, Germany

DH

338.
479
1
HON

5001336927